ORACLE PL/SQL Interview Questions, Answers, and Explanations

ORACOOKBOOK.COM

Please visit our website at www.sapcookbook.com
© 2006 Equity Press all rights reserved.

ISBN 1-933804-21-1

TABLE OF CONTENTS

ORACLE PL/SQL Interview Questions, Answers, and Explanations

ORACOOKBOOK
Equity Press

☞ QUESTION 1

On DBMS METADATA.get_ddl

How do I copy constraints from remote database 'TEST' into local copy of these tables?

ERROR Description:

ERROR at line 1:
ORA-31603: object "ORDER_ITEMS" of type TABLE not found in schema "HAHMED2"
ORA-06512: at "SYS.DBMS_METADATA", line 1511
ORA-06512: at "SYS.DBMS_METADATA", line 1548
ORA-06512: at "SYS.DBMS_METADATA", line 1864
ORA-06512: at "SYS.DBMS_METADATA", line 2684
ORA-06512: at "SYS.DBMS_METADATA", line 4220
ORA-06512: at line 1
ORA-06512: at line 29

Using script as below:

DECLARE

V_TABLENAME all_tables.table_name%TYPE;
l_ddl varchar2(32000);
V_COPYTABLENAME all_tables.table_name%TYPE;
v_tableExists boolean := false;

CURSOR c1 is
SELECT table_name FROM all_tables WHERE dropped = 'NO' and owner = 'TEST';
CURSOR c2 Is
Select table_name FROM user_tables where dropped =

```
'NO';
sql_stmt varchar2(200);


BEGIN
FOR rec1 IN c1 LOOP
v_tablename := rec1.table_name;
for rec2 in c2 loop
if rec2.table_name = (rec1.table_name || '_COPY') then
v_tableExists := true;
end if;

END LOOP;
if v_tableExists = false then
execute immediate 'create table ' || v_tablename || '_COPY as
select * from brendan.' || v_tablename;

---CONSTRAINT COPY ----
SELECT     DBMS_METADATA.GET_DDL     ('TABLE',     v_
tablename)
INTO v_copytablename
FROM all_tables
where owner='TEST';

---TRIGGERS COPY -------
For trg in (select trigger_name from all_triggers where
owner= 'BRENDAN' and table_name = v_tablename ) loop
l_ddl:=          cast(replace(replace(dbms_metadata.get_
ddl(     'TRIGGER',     trg.trigger_name),v_tablename,v_
copytablename),
trg.trigger_name,substr(v_copytablename||trg.trigger_
name, 1 , 30)) as varchar2);
execute immediate substr(l_ddl, 1, instr(l_ddl,'ALTER
TRIGGER')-1);
END LOOP;
```

END IF;
END LOOP;
END;

✍ ANSWER

If the schema listed have the table as below:

ORA-31603: object "ORDER_ITEMS" of type TABLE not found in schema "HAHMED2"

Do not select multiple calls/copies of get_ddl from all_tables especially since you are passing the same table name each time.

If it is not the same table name, you have not closed out of your outer loop. Please format your posts with appropriate code tags. Multiple results can't be used with a select into construct.

Try to avoid nested cursor for loops looping line by line in PLSQL, do things as single queries.

Better yet, go through the PLSQL user guide to become more familiar with the language. Try to write statements that generate SQL statements through the get_ddl calls, and have those written out to a file or the screen as a first step.

☞ QUESTION 2

Pipe select query

How can I perform a select operation on few tables in a DB, specifically placing a pipe (l) in between the column names and their corresponding data? The following is the kind of output I need:

JOB_IDlJOB_TITLElMIN_SALARYlMAX_SALARY   <--
Column Names
AD_PRESlPresidentl20000l40000
AD_VPlAdministration Vice Presidentl15000l30000
AD_ASSTlAdministration Assistantl3000l6000
FI_MGRlFinance Managerl8200l16000
FI_ACCOUNTlAccountantl4200l9000
...
...
...

✍ ANSWER

Spool it to a file and do a batch conversion. Another option would be string concatenation:

SQL> select the_value
  2   from (SELECT concat_all(concat_expr(column_
name,'l')) the_value
  3   , 1 rnk
  4   FROM user_tab_columns
  5   WHERE table_name = 'JOBS'
  6   UNION ALL

```
7   SELECT job_id||'|'||job_title||'|'||min_salary||'|'||max_ salary
    the_value
8   , 2 rnk
9   FROM  jobs
10  ORDER BY rnk
11
12 /
```
THE_VALUE

JOB_ID|JOB_TITLE|MIN_SALARY|MAX_SALARY
AD_PRES|President|20000|40000
AD_VP|Administration Vice President|15000|30000
AD_ASST|Administration Assistant|3000|6000
FI_MGR|Finance Manager|8200|16000
FI_ACCOUNT|Accountant|4200|9000
AC_MGR|Accounting Manager|8200|16000
AC_ACCOUNT|Public Accountant|4200|9000
SA_MAN|Sales Manager|10000|20000
SA_REP|Sales Representative|6000|12000
PU_MAN|Purchasing Manager|8000|15000
PU_CLERK|Purchasing Clerk|2500|5500
ST_MAN|Stock Manager|5500|8500
ST_CLERK|Stock Clerk|2000|5000
SH_CLERK|Shipping Clerk|2500|5500
IT_PROG|Programmer|4000|10000
MK_MAN|Marketing Manager|9000|15000
MK_REP|Marketing Representative|4000|9000
HR_REP|Human Resources Representative|4000|9000
PR_REP|Public Relations Representative|4500|10500

In order to get the concatenation string for the second part, use a slightly modified version of the first part:

SQL>   SELECT   concat_all(concat_expr(column_
name,'||'|'||')) the_value

```
2 FROM  user_tab_columns
3 WHERE  table_name = 'JOBS'
4 /
```
THE_VALUE

JOB_ID||'|'||JOB_TITLE||'|'||MIN_SALARY||'|'||MAX_SALARY

Another variant of concatenation is called STRAGG. The
numeric and date columns should have a TO_CHAR wrapped
around them. A decode could solve that:

```
SQL> SELECT concat_all(concat_expr(decode( data_type
2                      ,'VARCHAR2', column_name
3                      ,'TO_CHAR('||column_name||')'
4                      )
5              , '||"|"||')) the_value
6 FROM  user_tab_columns
7 WHERE  table_name = 'JOBS'
8 /
```

THE_VALUE

JOB_ID||'|'||JOB_TITLE||'|'||TO_CHAR(MIN_
SALARY)||'|'||TO_CHAR(MAX_SALARY)

☞ QUESTION 3

ORA-29278: SMTP transient error: 421 Service not available

I need to know why I get an error after inputting the following:

```
SQL> l
1  BEGIN
2  demo_mail.mail(
3  sender => 'Me <qalandar.hotmail.com>',
4  recipients => 'Someone <qalandar.gmail.com>, ' ||
5  '"Another one" <qalandark@hotmail.com>',
6  subject => 'Test',
7  message => 'Hi! This is a test.');
8* END;
SQL> /
```

ERROR at line 1:
ORA-29278: SMTP transient error: 421 Service not available
ORA-06512: at "SYS.UTL_SMTP", line 17
ORA-06512: at "SYS.UTL_SMTP", line 96
ORA-06512: at "SYS.UTL_SMTP", line 138

✍ ANSWER

Your server requires log-in information using UTL_SMTP. COMMAND (V_COON, 'AUTH LOGIN') where V_COON is connection variable. Give another two command lines for log-in and password.

☞ QUESTION 4

Multiple Row Updates

The table I am using has indexes but not on columns which are getting updated.

How do I make the process of making multiple row updates faster?

✍ ANSWER

Indexes on the columns being updated would render it even slower since oracle additionally needs to update the indexes (not only the table data).
Using indexes make data retrieval faster and since you have no WHERE clause in the UPDATE statement, it will always update every record in your table. Dividing your tables by dates, and having appropriate indexes and WHERE clause will help the process faster.

☞ QUESTION 5

Take Oracle dump

How do I take the contents of my database into an Excel sheet/spread sheet?

✍ ANSWER

You can create an ODBC connection directing towards your oracle database. Open Excel worksheet and click to get external data (import data). Use the ODBC connection to get database query and get all the data that you want into your excel worksheet.

☞ QUESTION 6

Parallel Query

I got a form where three long running queries are started successively by pressing a button. The queries are independent from each other.

Is there a way to start the three queries parallel on a single processor machine?

✍ ANSWER

Yes, but not exactly at the same time and surely not one after another. Use a scheduler which would run all three of them practically but you need time to do this.

☞ QUESTION 7

Copy data from .dat files to oracle?

How can I copy data from .dat files to oracle?

✍ ANSWER

You can choose either by using EXTERNAL TABLES or a "DTS" (Microsoft Data Transfer Service). Another possibility to do this is an SQL*Loader.

☞ QUESTION 8

Error while using dbms_lob.fileopen

Please help me to store an avi file on my database. I did the following but got an error response.

1- I've created a director name as 'sounds_dir'
2- I made a procedure to load the bfile:

```
-------------------------------------
create or replace procedure p_load (ploc varchar2)
is
vfile bfile;
begin
vfile := bfilename(ploc,'002.avi');
dbms_lob.fileopen(vfile);
dbms_lob.fileclose(vfile);
end;
-----------------------------------------
sql> execute p_load('sound_dir');
ERROR at line 1:
ORA-22285: non-existent  directory  or  file  for  FILEOPEN
operation
ORA-06512: at "SYS.DBMS_LOB", line 475
ORA-06512: at "SYS.P_LOAD", line 6
ORA-06512: at line 1
```

✍ ANSWER

SOUNDS_DIR must be in upper case, when you pass it to the procedure as a parameter. Like all other objects, by default, it is created in upper case.

scott@ORA92> create or replace directory sounds_dir as 'c:\ oracle'
 2 /

Directory created.

scott@ORA92> create or replace procedure p_load (ploc varchar2)
```
2      is
3      vfile bfile;
4      begin
5      vfile := bfilename(ploc,'002.avi');
6      dbms_lob.fileopen(vfile);
7      -- additional code to do something with it here
8      dbms_lob.fileclose(vfile);
9      exception
10     when others then dbms_lob.fileclose (vfile);
11     RAISE;
12     end;
13     /
```

Procedure created.

scott@ORA92> execute p_load('SOUNDS_DIR')

PL/SQL procedure successfully completed.

☞ QUESTION 9

Procedure execution hierarchy

I have an issue, wherein I need to find out procedure execution hierarchy.

Let's say Proc A call Proc B
Proc B call Proc C
Proc C call Proc D

In Proc D I encounter an exception, and I need to insert into an error table the hierarchy of the procedure calls, in the error message. I.e. I want to say "Encountered error in D: execution flow Is A.B.C.D"

How can I generate "A.B.C.D", without having to write extra code? Is there some internal table which I can use to figure the procedure execution hierarchy?

✍ ANSWER

You can use the Oracle supplied dbms_utility.foramt_call_stack, and/or Tom Kyte's who_am_i and who_called_me, available at:

http://asktom.oracle.com/~tkyte/who_called_me/index.html

Incorporate all three in the demonstration below.

scott@ORA92> CREATE TABLE error_tab
2   (who_am_i   VARCHAR2(61),
3   who_called_me VARCHAR2(61),

```
4       call_stack   CLOB)
5       /
```

Table created.

```
scott@ORA92>
scott@ORA92> CREATE OR REPLACE PROCEDURE d
2       AS
3       v_num   NUMBER;
4       v_owner         VARCHAR2(30);
5       v_name          VARCHAR2(30);
6       v_line    NUMBER;
7       v_caller_t VARCHAR2(100);
8       BEGIN
9       select to_number('a') into v_num from dual; -- cause
error for testing
10      EXCEPTION
11      WHEN OTHERS THEN
12      who_called_me (v_owner, v_name, v_line, v_caller_
t);
13      INSERT INTO error_tab
14      VALUES (who_am_i,
15              v_owner || '.' || v_name,
16               dbms_utility.format_call_stack);
17              END d;
18/
```

Procedure created.

```
scott@ORA92> SHOW ERRORS
No errors.
scott@ORA92> CREATE OR REPLACE PROCEDURE c
2       AS
3       EGIN
 4   d;
 5  END c;
```

```
  6 /
```

Procedure created.

```
scott@ORA92> CREATE OR REPLACE PROCEDURE b
  2  AS
  3  BEGIN
  4    c;
  5  END b;
  6 /
```

Procedure created.

```
scott@ORA92> CREATE OR REPLACE PROCEDURE a
  2  AS
  3  BEGIN
  4    b;
  5  END a;
  6 /
```

Procedure created.

scott@ORA92> execute a PL/SQL procedure successfully completed.

```
scott@ORA92> COLUMN who_am_i FORMAT A13
scott@ORA92> COLUMN who_called_me FORMAT A13
scott@ORA92> COLUMN call_stack    FORMAT A45
scott@ORA92> SELECT * FROM error_tab
  2 /
```

```
WHO_AM_I     WHO_CALLED_ME CALL_STACK
------------ ------------- ---------------------------------------------
SCOTT.D      SCOTT.C       ----- PL/SQL Call Stack -----
                          object   line  object
                          handle   number name
```

6623F488	1 anonymous block
66292138	13 procedure SCOTT.D
66299430	4 procedure SCOTT.C
6623D2F8	4 procedure SCOTT.B
6624F994	4 procedure SCOTT.A
66299984	1 anonymous block

To make a few quick modifications to Tom Kyte's who_called_ me procedure to create a flow function that is close to what you asked for, include revised demonstration below.

```
scott@ORA92> CREATE TABLE error_tab
2       (who_am_i     VARCHAR2(61),
3       who_called_me VARCHAR2(61),
4       flow          VARCHAR2(2000),
5       call_stack    CLOB)
6    /
```

Table created.

```
scott@ORA92> create or replace function flow
2       return     varchar2
3       as
4       call_stack    varchar2(4096)  default  dbms_utility.
format_call_stack;
5       n             number;
6       found_stack BOOLEAN default FALSE;
7       line          varchar2(255);
8       cnt           number := 0;
9       v_flow        varchar2(2000);
10      caller_t      varchar2(30);
11      owner         varchar2(30);
12      name          varchar2(30);
13      lineno        number;
14 begin
```

```
15 --
16      loop
17          n := instr( call_stack, chr(10) );
18          exit when ( n is NULL or n = 0 );
19 --
20          line := substr( call_stack, 1, n-1 );
21          call_stack := substr( call_stack, n+1 );
22 --
23          if ( NOT found_stack ) then
24              if ( line like '%handle%number%name%' )
then
25                  found_stack := TRUE;
26              end if;
27          else
28              cnt := cnt + 1;
29              -- cnt = 1 is ME
30              -- cnt = 2 is MY Caller
31              -- cnt = 3 is Their Caller
32              if ( cnt >= 2 ) then
33                  lineno := to_number(substr( line, 13, 6 ));
34                  line   := substr( line, 21 );
35                  if ( line like 'pr%' ) then
36                      n := length( 'procedure ' );
37                  elsif ( line like 'fun%' ) then
38                      n := length( 'function ' );
39                  elsif ( line like 'package body%' ) then
40                      n := length( 'package body ' );
41                  elsif ( line like 'pack%' ) then
42                      n := length( 'package ' );
43                  elsif ( line like 'anonymous%' ) then
44                      n := length( 'anonymous block ' );
45                  else
46                      n := null;
47                  end if;
48                  if ( n is not null ) then
49                      caller_t := ltrim(rtrim(upper(substr(
```

line, 1, n-1))));
50   else
51   caller_t := 'TRIGGER';
52   end if;
53
54   line := substr(line, nvl(n,1));
55   n := instr(line, '.');
56   owner := ltrim(rtrim(substr(line, 1, n-1
))));
57   name := ltrim(rtrim(substr(line, n+1)));
58   v_flow := v_flow || '->' || caller_t || ' ' || owner
|| '.' || name;
59   end if;
60   end if;
61   end loop;
62   return ltrim (v_flow, '->');
63 end;
64 /

Function created.

scott@ORA92> show errors
No errors.
scott@ORA92>
scott@ORA92> CREATE OR REPLACE PROCEDURE d
 2 AS
 3 v_num   NUMBER;
 4 v_owner   VARCHAR2(30);
 5 v_name   VARCHAR2(30);
 6 v_line   NUMBER;
 7 v_caller_t VARCHAR2(100);
 8 BEGIN
 9   select to_number('a') into v_num from dual; -- cause
error for testing
10 EXCEPTION
11   WHEN OTHERS THEN

```
12        who_called_me (v_owner, v_name, v_line, v_caller_
t);
13        INSERT INTO error_tab
14        VALUES (who_am_i,
15              v_owner || '.' || v_name,
16              flow,
17              dbms_utility.format_call_stack);
18  END d;
19  /
```

Procedure created.

scott@ORA92> SHOW ERRORS
No errors.
scott@ORA92> CREATE OR REPLACE PROCEDURE c
```
2  AS
3  BEGIN
4    d;
5  END c;
6  /
```

Procedure created.

scott@ORA92> CREATE OR REPLACE PROCEDURE b
```
2  AS
3  BEGIN
4    c;
5  END b;
6  /
```

Procedure created.

scott@ORA92> CREATE OR REPLACE PROCEDURE a
```
2  AS
3  BEGIN
4    b;
```

```
5  END a;
6  /
```

Procedure created.

scott@ORA92> execute a

PL/SQL procedure successfully completed.

```
scott@ORA92> COLUMN who_am_i FORMAT A13
scott@ORA92> COLUMN who_called_me FORMAT A13
scott@ORA92> COLUMN call_stack    FORMAT A45
scott@ORA92> SELECT * FROM error_tab
  2  /
```

WHO_AM_I   WHO_CALLED_ME
------------ ------------
FLOW

CALL_STACK

SCOTT.D   SCOTT.C
PROCEDURE   SCOTT.D->PROCEDURE   SCOTT.C-
>PROCEDURE   SCOTT.B->PROCEDURE   SCOTT.A-
>ANONYMOUS BLOCK .
----- PL/SQL Call Stack -----
  object   line object
  handle   number name
661B83F8   1 anonymous block
661C8564   13 procedure SCOTT.D
661B3C44   4 procedure SCOTT.C
661AA128   4 procedure SCOTT.B
661B909C   4 procedure SCOTT.A
66299984   1 anonymous block

☞ QUESTION 10

Genius trigger thoughts needed

I want to save data to a table (TBLSDSHIPMENTS) after a new record is saved in table (SHIPPER_LINE). Because of other triggers and restrictions on this table, I am not able to save all the data I need to a table with an after insert trigger.

Some of the critical fields that are needed can be saved but not all. I have used a vb app with a timer to monitor a table and perform the updates. Is there a work-around or timer that can be used to go in, check and populate the TBLSDSHIPMENTS table?

✎ ANSWER

The design is flawed if this is a real world business requirement. Always implement a private JOB_QUEUE table that is updated by the INSERT trigger and processed later by a real DBMS_JOB entry.

☞ QUESTION 11

Reading a string from a file until end of line

There is a flat file "param.txt" which has got some parameters set in it. (no repetitions of parameter-name)

...<param1>......................
...<param2>.... ....
....
Recipient a@b.com, c@d.com
....
...<paramn>....................

I have to open param.txt and search for "Recipient" word, and then copy the words thereafter until end-of-line (i.e., the email addresses).

How do I call (and pass arguments to) a java method from a PL/SQL procedure?

✍ ANSWER

Using UTL_FILE built-in package can perform file I/O. Check the documentation or search the web, there are plenty of examples.

If possible you could use the file as an external table.

You can't just call a method of an externally running java application. You can write a stored procedure in java (which is stored in the database as pl/sql and is running in the oracle's internal JVM). You can't "communicate" with a JVM running on the oracle's host system.

☞ QUESTION 12

Pass the parameter to the cursor

Kindly refer to procedure below and help find any mistakes that I have done. How do I pass the parameter to the cursor? Creating the cursor only will take the value and create, or while opening the cursor, the value will be taken and data will be fetched. Help me find the solution to this.

create or replace PROCEDURE S_vid AS
SUP_CODE VARCHAR2(8);
SUP_NAME VARCHAR2(28);
ITM_CODE VARCHAR2(10);
ITM_DESC1 VARCHAR2(24);
ITM_DESC2 VARCHAR2(24);
FAC_CODE VARCHAR2(9);
FAC_NAME VARCHAR2(28);
DISP_INDENT NUMBER(20,3);
sin_st_date date;
sin_end_date date;
day1 varchar2(9);
CURSOR SCOMP(s_st_date date,s_end_date date) IS
SELECT   SIN_SUP_CODE,SUP_NAME,SIN_ITM_
CODE,ITM_DESCRIPTION1,
ITM_DESCRIPTION2,SIN_FAC_CODE,FAC_
NAME,SUM(SIN_DISP_INDENT)
FROM
SUP_INDENT,SUP_MSTR, FSI_REF, ITM_MSTR, FAC_
MSTR
WHERE
SIN_IND_DATE >= TO_DATE(TO_CHAR(s_st_date,'DD-
MON-YYYY')) AND
SIN_IND_DATE <= TO_DATE(TO_CHAR(s_end_date,'DD-

MON-YYYY')) AND
SIN_FAC_CODE = FSI_FAC_CODE AND
SIN_ITM_CODE = FSI_ITM_CODE AND
SIN_SUP_CODE = FSI_SUP_CODE AND
SIN_DISP_INDENT > 0 AND
SIN_FAC_CODE = FAC_CODE AND
SIN_ITM_CODE = ITM_CODE AND
SIN_SUP_CODE = SUP_CODE AND
SUP_PC_CODE = 'PP' AND
ITM_PC_CODE = 'PP'
GROUP BY
SIN_SUP_CODE, SUP_NAME, SIN_ITM_CODE,ITM_
DESCRIPTION1, ITM_DESCRIPTION2, SIN_FAC_
CODE,FAC_NAME;
BEGIN
select to_char(sysdate,'DAY') into day1 from dual;
if day1 = 'WEDNESDAY' then
select sysdate - 5 into sin_st_date from dual;
select sysdate+1 into sin_end_date from dual;
elsif day1 = 'THURSDAY' then
select sysdate - 6 into sin_st_date from dual;
select sysdate into sin_end_date from dual;
end if;
OPEN SCOMP(sin_st_date,sin_end_date);
DBMS_OUTPUT.ENABLE(1000000);
DBMS_OUTPUT.PUT_LINE('"SUP_CODE","SUP_
NAME","ITM_CODE","ITM_DESCRIPTION","FAC_
CODE","FAC_NAME","DISPATCH_INDENT"');
LOOP
FETCH SCOMP INTO SUP_CODE, SUP_NAME, ITM_
CODE,
ITM_DESC1, ITM_DESC2, FAC_CODE, FAC_NAME, DISP_
INDENT;
EXIT WHEN SCOMP%NOTFOUND;
DBMS_OUTPUT.PUT_LINE('"'||SUP_CODE||'","'||SUP_

NAME||'",'"||ITM_CODE||'",'"||ITM_DESC1||'   '||ITM_
DESC2||'",'"|| FAC_CODE||'",'"||FAC_NAME||'",'"||DISP_
INDENT||'",'||FAC_CODE||SUP_CODE||ITM_CODE);
END LOOP;
END;

✍ ANSWER

Although unformatted, it appears that procedure is correctly written (i.e. doesn't have syntax errors).

Why doesn't it return any records?   As you enabled SERVEROUTPUT, perhaps cursor isn't fetching anything. Besides, as it is Thursday here (where I live), this code will work for several more hours.   What then and what values will 'sin_st_date' and 'sin_end_date' have tomorrow?   Is the procedure designed to be run on Wednesdays and/or Thursdays?

Try it with.....

select to_char(sysdate,'fmDAY') into day1 from dual;

OR

select trim(to_char(sysdate,'DAY')) into day1 from dual;

instead of

select to_char(sysdate,'DAY') into day1 from dual;

because..

>SELECT TO_CHAR(SYSDATE,'DAY')||'!!!' FROM dual;

TO_CHAR(SYSD

THURSDAY !!!

>SELECT TO_CHAR(SYSDATE,'fmDAY')||'!!!' FROM dual;

TO_CHAR(SYSD

THURSDAY!!!

Another possible solution will be to truncate a date to remove the time portion. Furthermore, TO_DATE without an explicit DATE format is not very robust coding.

It seems you are querying from past Friday to next Thursday. You could rewrite the query using sysdate or TRUNC(sysdate) in your case, and the NEXT_DAY built-in to fetch the next Thursday. Start_date would be NEXT_DAY(TRUNC(SYSDATE-7),'FRI') and stop_date would be NEXT_DAY(TRUNC(SYSDATE-1),'THU'). No need for IF constructions.

☞ QUESTION **13**

TRIGGER 9i – CLEAR or REVERT

I have a 9i AFTER INSERT trigger below which populates another table only if a condition is met. I need to CLEAR or REVERT the prior trigger commands if that condition (IF mCUSTOMER_ID='97' AND mUSER_SHIPPED_QTY >0) is not met. Other triggers on the table are not saving a record in this table, due to my trigger.

```
DECLARE
mSHIPPED_DATE          SYSADM.SHIPPER.SHIPPED_
DATE%type;
mPACKLIST_ID SYSADM.SHIPPER.PACKLIST_ID%type;
mLINE_NO SYSADM.SHIPPER_LINE.LINE_NO%type;
mCUST_ORDER_ID         SYSADM.SHIPPER_LINE.CUST_
ORDER_ID%type;
mCUST_ORDER_LINE_NO        SYSADM.SHIPPER_LINE.
CUST_ORDER_LINE_NO%type;
mORDER_QTY      SYSADM.CUST_ORDER_LINE.ORDER_
QTY%type;
mUSER_SHIPPED_QTY   SYSADM.SHIPPER_LINE.USER_
SHIPPED_QTY%type;
mQTY_BO varchar2(10);
mDESCRIPTION SYSADM.PART.DESCRIPTION%type;
mCUSTOMER_ID           SYSADM.CUSTOMER_ORDER.
CUSTOMER_ID%type;
mCUSTOMER_PO_REF    SYSADM.CUSTOMER_ORDER.
CUSTOMER_PO_REF%type;
mSHIPPED_TIME varchar2(30);
mseqNo NUMBER;
mPART_ID SYSADM.CUST_ORDER_LINE.PART_ID%type;
mTOTALSHIPPEDQTY       SYSADM.CUST_ORDER_LINE.
```

```
TOTAL_SHIPPED_QTY%type;
PRAGMA AUTONOMOUS_TRANSACTION;

BEGIN

SELECT
SYSADM.SHIPPER.SHIPPED_DATE,
SYSADM.SHIPPER.PACKLIST_ID,
:OLDDATA.LINE_NO,
:OLDDATA.CUST_ORDER_ID,
:OLDDATA.CUST_ORDER_LINE_NO,
SYSADM.CUST_ORDER_LINE.ORDER_QTY,
:OLDDATA.USER_SHIPPED_QTY,
SYSADM.PART.DESCRIPTION,
SYSADM.CUSTOMER_ORDER.CUSTOMER_ID,
SYSADM.CUSTOMER_ORDER.CUSTOMER_PO_REF,
SYSADM.SHIPPER.SHIPPED_TIME,
SYSADM.CUST_ORDER_LINE.PART_ID,
SYSADM.CUST_ORDER_LINE.TOTAL_SHIPPED_QTY

INTO    mSHIPPED_DATE,    mPACKLIST_ID,    mLINE_
NO,    mCUST_ORDER_ID,    mCUST_ORDER_LINE_NO,
mORDER_QTY, mUSER_SHIPPED_QTY, mDESCRIPTION,
mCUSTOMER_ID, mCUSTOMER_PO_REF, mSHIPPED_
TIME, mPART_ID, mTOTALSHIPPEDQTY
FROM  SYSADM.SHIPPER, SYSADM.CUST_ORDER_LINE,
SYSADM.CUSTOMER_ORDER,    SYSADM.CUSTOMER,
SYSADM.PART
WHERE    SYSADM.SHIPPER.PACKLIST_ID=    :OLDDATA.
PACKLIST_ID
AND   :OLDDATA.CUST_ORDER_ID   =   SYSADM.CUST_
ORDER_LINE.CUST_ORDER_ID
AND   :OLDDATA.CUST_ORDER_LINE_NO   =   SYSADM.
CUST_ORDER_LINE.LINE_NO
AND    SYSADM.CUSTOMER_ORDER.CUSTOMER_ID    =
```

SYSADM.CUSTOMER.ID
AND SYSADM.CUST_ORDER_LINE.CUST_ORDER_ID =
SYSADM.CUSTOMER_ORDER.ID
AND SYSADM.CUST_ORDER_LINE.PART_ID = SYSADM.
PART.ID;
IF mCUSTOMER_ID='97' AND mUSER_SHIPPED_QTY >0
THEN
SELECT TBLSDSHIPMENTS_SEQUENCE.nextval INTO
mseqNo FROM dual;
INSERT INTO TBLSDSHIPMENTS (SDID, SHIPPED_DATE,
PACKLIST_ID, LINE_NO, CUST_ORDER_ID, CUST_
ORDER_LINE_NO, ORDER_QTY, USER_SHIPPED_QTY,
QTY_BO, DESCRIPTION, CUSTOMER_ID, CUSTOMER_
PO_REF, SHIPPED_TIME, SDSHIPMENTSTATUS, PART_
ID)
VALUES (mseqNo, mSHIPPED_DATE, mPACKLIST_ID,
mLINE_NO, mCUST_ORDER_ID, mCUST_ORDER_LINE_
NO, mORDER_QTY, mUSER_SHIPPED_QTY, mORDER_
QTY - (mTOTALSHIPPEDQTY + mUSER_SHIPPED_QTY),
mDESCRIPTION, mCUSTOMER_ID, mCUSTOMER_PO_
REF, SUBSTR(mSHIPPED_TIME,12,, 10, mPART_ID);
COMMIT;
END IF;
END;

I want none of the commands (lines) to affect the table if that condition is not met. For some reason now, even though the code above seems straight forward, another trigger on the table has a problem with my code and will not save a record in the table, even though this is an after insert trigger. I was hoping for some REVERT, or CLEAR command that could be executed if the insert condition is not met.

The logic is to save a record to another table, (TBLSDSHIPMENTS) if the value of the inserted record and

related tables in this table is equal to
(IF mCUSTOMER_ID='97' AND mUSER_SHIPPED_QTY
>0).

This seems easy, but there are other triggers on the table (my table is based on) that my trigger is affecting. In some rare cases a record is not saved. I want to prevent my trigger logic affecting anything unless the above condition is met.

What is the best way to do this?

✍ ANSWER

If something in another trigger that is affected by the transaction fails, then the insert from your trigger will be rolled back. In most cases, that is the desired affect. If you want the insert to be committed, even if the rest of it fails, then you will need to use a commit with pragma autonomous_transaction. However, if the failure occurs before your trigger is fired, then your insert will never occur. Triggers fire in the order of: before statement, before row, after row, and after statement. Triggers at the same level may fire in any order. If you need to guarantee the order, then you need to put the logic in one trigger, or procedures that are called from one trigger.

☞ QUESTION 14

What kind of mistake is this?

What is causing an error if I have this procedure?

```
PROCEDURE wstawmysql1
  (tabela IN VARCHAR2)
 AS
   script  CLOB;
   script1 clob;
   nazwa varchar2(50);
   typ varchar2(50);
   Cursor_name INTEGER := DBMS_SQL.OPEN_CURSOR;
   ret  INTEGER;
   col1  VARCHAR2(2000);
   v_col_count INTEGER := 0;
   Cursor cur(c_tname varchar2) is
    select column_name,data_type from user_tab_columns
where lower(table_name)=lower(c_tname);
  BEGIN
   -- ddl
      script := 'Create table ' || tabela || '(' || CHR(13) ||
CHR(10);
   open cur(tabela);
    loop
    fetch cur into nazwa,typ;
   exit when cur%notfound;
   if typ='VARCHAR2' then typ:='varchar(255)';
   end if;
   if typ='NUMBER' then typ:='INT';
   end if;
   script:=script||nazwa||' '||typ||','||CHR(13)||CHR(10);
   end loop;
```

```
close cur;
script:=script||');';
script1:=substr(script,1,length(script)-5);
script:=script1||');' || CHR(13) || CHR(10);


   DBMS_SQL.PARSE (cursor_name, 'SELECT * FROM ' ||
tabela, DBMS_SQL.NATIVE);
   FOR i IN 1 .. 255 LOOP
   BEGIN
       DBMS_SQL.DEFINE_COLUMN (cursor_name, i, col1,
2000);
   v_col_count := i;
   EXCEPTION
     WHEN OTHERS THEN
     IF SQLCODE = -1007 THEN EXIT;
     ELSE RAISE;
     END IF;
   END;
   END LOOP;
       DBMS_SQL.DEFINE_COLUMN (cursor_name, 1, col1,
2000);
   ret := DBMS_SQL.EXECUTE (cursor_name);
   LOOP
 EXIT WHEN DBMS_SQL.FETCH_ROWS (cursor_name) <=
0;
   script := script || 'INSERT INTO ' || tabela || ' VALUES (';
   FOR i IN 1 .. v_col_count LOOP
     DBMS_SQL.COLUMN_VALUE (cursor_name, i, col1);
     script := script || '''' || REPLACE (col1, '''', '''''') || '''' || ',';
   END LOOP;
   script := SUBSTR (script, 1, LENGTH (script) - 1) || ');' ||
CHR(13) || CHR(10);
   END LOOP;
   DBMS_SQL.CLOSE_CURSOR (cursor_name);
```

-- delete from xmltab and insert scripts into xmltab:
DELETE from xmltab;
INSERT INTO xmltab VALUES (19, script);
commit;
END wstawmysql1;

When I run it on a smaller table, all is good. But when I run the procedure for a bigger table, for example 600 rows and 17 columns, procedure works longer and returns with this mistake:

ORA-01652: unable to extend temp segment by 128 in tablespace TEMP

Another problem I would encounter is when the table has more columns (about 12 or more). My procedure creates me a ddl script with the same columns, but in different order. for example; table has these columns 1,2,3,4,5,6, but procedure create this ddl 4,1,2,3,5,6 etc.

✍ ANSWER

You are out of space in TEMP tablespace. Either add more space or make your query do less sorting. Check if somebody was doing a large index build at that time. Without using an ORDER BY clause, do not expect Oracle to know what order to return your select statement, hence the different order each time you run it. This is a classic mistake by people who do not fully grasp what a relational database is.

☞ QUESTION 15

Put 30+ select stmts in 1 proc with 1 refcursor

I have about 30+ queries in Oracle and I need to write a stored procedure that will return a refcursor.

Procedure will have User ID as input parameter and will be passed in a string of numbers that are comma delimited and refcursor as output.

All 30 + queries return different data.

I have created a temporary table Temp_Table.

First procedure (phase 1) will be executed to empty the temp table.

In the next step (phase II), information from the 30+ individual queries would be stored in a single row for each user id within that Temporary table.

I want to use 30+ variables to store the results of each individual query for each individual User ID. My understanding is I should not have to use a cursor at this point.

After all the queries have been performed, the variables would be used to insert the results into the temp table for the individual users being processed.

The last phase (phase III), the Stored Procedure would be creating a "single" Ref Cursor. The structure of the cursor would be the results of the 30+ individual queries contained in the temporary table.

What I am doing right now is:

PROCEDURE USERID_PROC(p_user_id IN NUMBER, c_get_data OUT c_get_typ);

At first, I was using

r_get_data c_get_typ;

LOOP
OPEN c_get_date for
SELECT.........

FETCH INTO
EXIT WHEN c_get_data%NOTFOUND;
CLOSE c_get_data;

END LOOP;

this way, I will have to declare 30+ cursors for 30 + queries.

Or; should I use:

MERGE INTO TEMP_TABLE t
USING (
select ....
ON (
t.user_id = v_outage_skey) -- declared variable
WHEN MATCHED
THEN ?????????????
-- DO NOTHING b/c we don't want to insert duplicate records

WHEN NOT MATCHED
THEN INSERT

values (......);

and then declare a cursor

OPEN CURSOR FOR
select * from cursor -- TO GET DATA FROM THE TABLE

Is this approach correct? If not, what should I do?

✍ ANSWER

You can do this even without creating a temporary table using UNION operator. Just construct a select statement with Union operator and open a cursor for that select stmt.

For example:

SELECT A.col1, A.col2, A.col3 from A WHERE A.col4 = 'xxx'
UNION
SELECT B.col1, B.col2, B.col3 from B WHERE B.col4 = 123
UNION
SELECT C.col1, C.col2, C.col3 from C WHERE C.col4 is null
UNION
....
....
....
....
....
so on..

ORACLE PL/SQL Interview Questions, Answers, and Explanations

☞ QUESTION 16

Function to return database name

I need to write a PL/SQL function that returns the database name so that the user that calls the function will be connected to it.

The select return that I need is:

"SELECT name FROM v$DATABASE";

However, if I wrap the select into function, I get the table or view does not exist error. The function I test with is:

FUNCTION SID RETURN VARCHAR2 IS

CURSOR NEXT_id IS SELECT name FROM v$DATABASE;
RET varchar2(254);

BEGIN
open NEXT_ID;
FETCH NEXT_id INTO RET;
CLOSE NEXT_id;
RETURN RET;
END SID;

✍ ANSWER

It's a classic: the grant on V$DATABASE is given through a ROLE. Get the grant directly or make the procedure run under invokers' rights. You can also use:
SYS_CONTEXT('USERENV','DB_NAME')

SELECT sys_context('USERENV','DB_NAME')
FROM dual;

Or;

SELECT
SYS.DATABASE_NAME
FROM
DUAL;

☞ QUESTION 17

Default permission for files written by UTL_FILE

Do you know if a file is written by UTL_FILE in the utl_file_dir directory by the oracle user, and what permission it has? If the procedure is run by a different user, does it depend on the umask of that user or is it a default?

✍ ANSWER

On UNIX systems, the owner of a file created by the FOPEN function is the owner of the shadow process running the instance. Normally, the owner is ORACLE. Files created using FOPEN are always writable and readable using the UTL_FILE subprograms, but non privileged users who need to read these files, outside of PL/SQL, may need access from a system administrator.

You can also try to set utl_file_dir path into init.ora file. Then you can call UTL_FILE package.

☞ QUESTION 18

Separating values from string

I get one comma string like '2,3,4,5,6'.
In function I am separating these values.
My functions are as follows;

```
create or replace function str2tbl( p_str in varchar2 ) return
number
 as
   l_str   long default p_str || ',';
   l_n       number;
   l_data   number;
   l_data1   number;
 begin
   loop
     l_n := instr( l_str, ',' );
     exit when (nvl(l_n,0) = 0);
     --l_data.extend;
     l_data := ltrim(rtrim(substr(l_str,1,l_n-1)));
     l_str := substr( l_str, l_n+1 );
     l_data1 := l_data;
   end loop;
   return l_data1;
end;
```

The above functions are not working well. I need help.

✍ ANSWER

You have not copied and pasted as you should have. You are
missing a user defined type. Your function does not return
one number but rather it is returning a series of numbers.

On my box, it exists as STRING_TO_TAB and it looks like this:

```
SQL> desc string_to_tab
FUNCTION string_to_tab RETURNS VC2_TAB
 Argument Name          Type              In/Out Default?
 --------------------- ------------------- ------ --------
 PIV_STRING            VARCHAR2            IN
 PIV_DELIMITER         VARCHAR2             IN

SQL> desc vc2_tab
 vc2_tab TABLE OF VC2_TYPE
 Name                       Null?   Type
 -------------------------- ------- ------------------------
 THE_VALUE                          VARCHAR2(255)

SQL> desc vc2_type
 Name                       Null?   Type
 -------------------------- ------- ------------------------
 THE_VALUE                          VARCHAR2(255)

SQL> select the_value
  2    from table(string_to_tab('1,2,3,4,5,6,7,8',','))
  3  /

THE_VALUE
-----------------------------------------------------------------
1
2
3
4
5
6
7
8
```

You have one scalar type (not really necessary but I use it to name my column); one tabular type, and one table function returning this table type. In SQL, you can use the TABLE() keyword to get the output as rows.

☞ QUESTION **19**

Procedures under package

How can I view all procedures of a package in a DBMS_PIPE package?

✍ ANSWER

You can view the procedures of a package through:

"DESCRIBE DBMS_PIPEor"; when all else fails, read the documentation and re-write configuration.

☞ QUESTION 20

Executing shell scripts and other UNIX commands

I am working on a project that would be a great benefit, if I was able to create a stored procedure that would execute a shell script or other types of UNIX commands. There does not seem to be any documentation on this problem.

Is this possible at all?

✍ ANSWER

Go to http://download-west.oracle.com/docs/cd/B10501_01/ You can use DBMS_PIPE package to pipe whatever you need to a UNIX shell script. Just make the shell script wait on this pipe. Also, in Oracle 10g, you can use DBMS_SCHEDULER. Pre-10g. You can also do it with a dynamically linked C program that performs the system.

☞ QUESTION 21

Renaming image

I want to create functionality for save image 1.jpg as 2.jpg on the server.

Can this be done from any procedure or function written in the database?

If yes, how can I rename the image stored on server?

✍ ANSWER

You can save files in the database in BLOB columns. To manipulate images, you must create an application. Take note that when you save an image in the database, you save them without any name, simply in the column COL_NAME.

☞ QUESTION **22**

Trigger Problem

I have a problem with the following trigger:

```
create or replace trigger t_test_match
before insert on test_table
for each row
declare
v_ex exception;
begin
if (owa_pattern.match(:new.firstname,'^[a-z,A-Z]{1,10}$'))
then
  null;
else
 raise v_ex;
end if;
exception
when v_ex then
RAISE_APPLICATION_ERROR(-20001,'wrong    values    in
firstname');
when others then
RAISE_APPLICATION_ERROR(-20003, 'Unknown  error!' ||
SQLERRM);
end t_test_match;
/
```

Everything works right if I do an insert like this:

```
insert into test_table (firstname)
values('hugo');
```

But errors occur when I try to insert this:

insert into test_table (firstname)
values('hugo35');

ORA-06512: at "user.t_test_match", line
12
ORA-04088: error during execution of trigger
'user.t_test_match'

Is this normal or were there errors committed?

✍ ANSWER

The other two lines are the callstack. It indicates the route how the code in which the error occurred was called. Normally the calling code (i.e. your application) would handle the error. You would not see the other lines.

If you write this trigger for name validation, then it works, but if you add a number with the string then you have to change it as:
'^[a-z,A-Z,0-9]{1,10}$'

Your input name must not have spaces.

☞ QUESTION **23**

AUTHID CURRENT_USER

When I call a procedure A with AUTHID CURRENT_USER, which in turn calls procedure B with AUTHID DEFINER, then there is a switch from current user to definer user. When we have it the other way around, (for example: I call a procedure A with AUTHID DEFINER, which in turn calls procedure B with AUTHID CURRENT_USER), is the DEFINER USER carried over even when procedure B is executed?

Is this a feature or a Bug?

✍ ANSWER

That is a feature. If A is running as DEFINER and it calls B (CURRENT_USER), then as far as B is concerned, the definer of A is the current user.

☞ Question 24

Comparing numeric arrays

I have two numeric range arrays A and B. I have to compare and get the numbers that are present in A, and not present in B. Do we have any direct method in PL/SQL (not loops) which can be used directly?

The purpose is to know if I can do the same activity in JAVA and pass it to the procedure for further actions, or do it in the procedure itself.

Example

A:: [1-100,200-300,150-400]
B:: [50-150,220-300]

The output must be individually numbered in A that is not present in B.

✍ Answer

You can use the MUTISET_EXCEPT operator in 10g.

CREATE TYPE num_tab AS TABLE OF INTEGER;Load the numbers into two Nested Tables (a and b) of type NUM_TAB
SELECT a MULTISET_EXCEPT b
INTO   c
FROM   dual;

It could also be done as a MINUS of two TABLE()

functions.
```
SELECT CAST(MULTISET(
  SELECT COLUMN_VALUE
  FROM TABLE(a)
  MINUS
  SELECT COLUMN_VALUE
  FROM TABLE(b)
) AS num_tab
FROM dual
```

Please check syntax again.

☞ QUESTION **25**

PLSQL PERF CHALLENGE: Tree traversing to calc an expression recursive dependence of variables

We are writing a set of procedures and functions to return the value of an expression, based on a variable which in turn can be based on other variables.

Here is an example of a simple tree showing dependencies:
VARIABLE V1 can be calculated by traversing the following:
> [V2]/4*(1+15/100)
>>>>>> 2.75
>>>>>> [V3]*1.05
>>>>>> [V4]
>>>>>>>>>> [V3]*3
>>>>>>>>>> 100
> 2*[V3]+75
> 10+9

With V3=5 for example.

V3 is being the only variable directly assigned.
We are trying to solve the problem with PL/SQL recursion.

Does performance of PL/SQL become an issue when we have to do this on more than 20,000 records, each based on a variable based on others with an average tree depth of 4 levels?

✍ ANSWER

Basically, I will be using recursion and a function to calculate the expression after variable has been replaced by its value. Each expression can only use ONE variable.

Recursive function looks like:

CREATE OR REPLACE FUNCTION Es_Calc_rate (VAR Varchar2, lvl number:=1) RETURN NUMBER IS

CURSOR c1 (Parent_Var Varchar2) IS

SELECT Var_Code_used,UnitCost,Formula,Nature FROM exp_buildup

WHERE Var_Code = Parent_VarCode;

K NUMBER:=0;

BEGIN

FOR R in c1 (RESCODE) LOOP

/* RECURSIVE CALL For All Sub levels underneath Root */

Es_Calc_rate(R.Var_code_Used,lvl+1);

/* To be First In Last out executed */

/* expression calc etc.. Still in progress */

END LOOP;

END;

/

Expression Calc function:

Use "EXECUTE IMMEDIATE 'select '||EXPR||' fro dual' into RESULT" statement to process a formula after variable has been replaced.

This should be enough to get a clear idea to write and achieve reasonable PERF.

☞ QUESTION 26

Error Message

I would like to create a query which I can use in Oracle form report, to select dates between periods. I created a code list below:

SELECT equipment.equipment_id, equipment_schedule. equipment_id, function.function_no, equipment_schedule. function_no, equipment_name, function_name, function_ date
FROM equipment, function, equipment_schedule
WHERE function.function_no = equipment_schedule. function_no
AND equipment.equipment_id = equipment_schedule. equipment_id
AND function_date = :function_date(select * from function where function_date between
'01-JUL-2005' AND '02-JUL-2005');

But it gave me error like this: SP2-0552: Bind variable "FUNCTION_DATE" not declared.

I do not understand this. Please help.

✍ ANSWER

Reading your post, it will be enough to substitute the whole sub query with either of these:

AND function_date BETWEEN '01-JUL-2005' AND '02-JUL-2005'

[Updated on: Wed, 08 March 2006 01:30];

Or;

AND function_date BETWEEN to_date('01-JUL-2005', 'dd-mon-yyyy') AND to_date('02-JUL-2005', 'dd-mon-yyyy');

☞ QUESTION 27

Creating or Locating Efficient Function

I have created a cursor to populate a numeric sequence-like field per record ID.
I am thinking that there is a more efficient way to do this, perhaps a function. I'm sure this is a common task.

An Example of output is:
ID: COUNT:
R1 1
R1 2
R2 1
R2 2
R3 3

My cursor is:


```
DECLARE
vcCnt   NUMBER;
vcCntr   NUMBER;
vcMemID              VARCHAR2(20);
CURSOR c IS
SELECT DISTINCT memberid FROM eob_re2;
BEGIN

        FOR crec in c LOOP

        SELECT COUNT(memberid) INTO vcCnt
        FROM eob_re2
        WHERE memberid = crec.memberid;
```

```
vcCntr := 0;

WHILE vcCntr <= vcCnt

    LOOP

        INSERT INTO cjs_temp1
        (memid, count)
        VALUES (crec.memberid, vcCntr);

        vcCntr := vcCntr + 1;

    END LOOP;
END LOOP;
COMMIT;
END;
/
```

✍ ANSWER

No function or procedural/looping code needed. Just a single SQL statement:

```
insert into cjs_temp1 (memid, count)
    select memberid, row_number() over (partition by memberid order by null)
    from eob_re2;
```

Your sample code started the counter at 0 but your desired output started at 1. The above statement will start at 1, change if necessary.

☞ QUESTION **28**

Regarding output generation

I was writing a code but a procedure was created. I received some errors when I executed that procedure. Sample code as follows:

```
1 create or replace procedure hello1(p_empno in number) is
2 v_emp emp%rowtype;
3 begin
4 SELECT *
5 INTO v_emp
6 FROM emp
7 WHERE empno = p_empno;
8 OWA_UTIL.Mime_Header('text/xml');
9 HTP.Print(
10 '<?xml version="1.0"?>'
11 || '<EMP>'
12 || ' <EMPNO>'||v_emp.empno||'</EMPNO>'
13 || ' <ENAME>'||v_emp.ename||'</ENAME>'
14 || ' <DEPTNO>'||v_emp.deptno||'</DEPTNO>'
15 || ' <SAL>'||v_emp.sal||'</SAL>'
16 || '</EMP>');
17 EXCEPTION
18 WHEN OTHERS THEN
19 OWA_UTIL.Mime_Header('text/xml');
20 HTP.Print(
21 '<?xml version="1.0"?>'
22 || '<ROWSET>'
23 || ' <ERROR>'||SQLERRM||'</ERROR>'
24 || '</ROWSET>');
25* END;
```

26 /

Procedure created.

SQL> exec hello1(7369);
BEGIN hello1(7369); END;

*

ERROR at line 1:
ORA-06502: PL/SQL: numeric or value error
ORA-06512: at "SYS.OWA_UTIL", line 323
ORA-06512: at "SYS.OWA_UTIL", line 364
ORA-06512: at "SCOTT.HELLO1", line 19
ORA-06502: PL/SQL: numeric or value error
ORA-06512: at line 1

I need some clarification on the above procedure.

✍ ANSWER

The sqlerrm in your exception part should be: to_
char(sqlerrm).
There is also something wrong with a line of your code.

Quote:
OWA_UTIL.Mime_Header('text/xml');

(Please check the pl/sql packages guide for details on this
package).

Please see the following:

1 create or replace procedure hello1(p_empno in number)
is

```
2 v_emp emp%rowtype;
3 begin
4 SELECT *
5 INTO v_emp
6 FROM emp
7 WHERE empno = p_empno;
8 OWA_UTIL.Mime_Header('text/xml');
9 HTP.Print(
10 '<?xml version="1.0"?>'
11 || '<EMP>'
12 || ' <EMPNO>'||v_emp.empno||'</EMPNO>'
13 || ' <ENAME>'||v_emp.ename||'</ENAME>'
14 || ' <DEPTNO>'||v_emp.deptno||'</DEPTNO>'
15 || ' <SAL>'||v_emp.sal||'</SAL>'
16 || '</EMP>');
17 EXCEPTION
18 WHEN OTHERS THEN
19 --OWA_UTIL.Mime_Header('text/xml');
20 HTP.Print(
21 '<?xml version="1.0"?>'
22 || '<ROWSET>'
23 || ' <ERROR>'||to_char(SQLERRM)||'</ERROR>'
24 || '</ROWSET>');
25* END;
SQL> /
```

Procedure created.

SQL> exec hello1(7369);

PL/SQL procedure successfully completed.

☞ QUESTION **29**

Execute windows copy cmd within PL/SQL block

Can anyone tell me how to execute a windows copy command within PL/SQL block? If possible, please provide some sample code. I need it for taking HOT backups.

✍ ANSWER

You can use utl_file.fcopy. Please see http://www.oracle.com/technology/oramag/oracle/02-sep/o52plsql.html, for an example.

Also for hot backups, there must be already a number of free utilities available. Perhaps you can take a look at them before making the efforts to write your own scripts.

☞ QUESTION 30

Suppress additional message lines in raise application error

Is it possible to suppress additional message lines that appear with raised application error? For example,

SQL> begin
2 raise_application_error(-20000,'Just checking');
3 end;
4 /
begin
*
ERROR at line 1:
ORA-20000: Just checking
ORA-06512: at line 2

I just want the ORA-20000 line, not the ORA-06512 line, etc. Of course, many times there may be additional lines also.

✍ ANSWER

That is Oracle's output format for unhandled errors. If you want to do something special, then you can HANDLE the exception:

declare
procedure do_something(code IN number, description IN VARCHAR2)
 as
 begin

```
   ....
   end;
 begin
 raise_application_error(-20000,'Just checking');
 exeception
   when others then
    do_something(sqlcode, sqlerrm);
 end;
 /
```

The block will return successfully (eg. PL/SQL procedure successfully completed.). Whatever you wanted to do upon error must be done in do_something.

☞ QUESTION 31

Regarding information about files

I have one doubt regarding UTL_FILE. How can you compare two files, and if there is an updated record in that file? That record will be put into a separate file.can. I have to write code in pl/sql.

Are there any method using cursors like this?

✍ ANSWER

If those are delimited files, then you can create external tables.
After that, it is simple to get the difference using minus and putting it in a file using UTL_FILE or a SELECT again.

Try this:

Place your delimited files emp1.txt and emp2.txt in /tmp
This is 9i feature.

Create directory personnel as '/tmp';

        CREATE TABLE emp_ext1
        (empcode NUMBER(4), empname VARCHAR2(25),
        job VARCHAR2(25))
        ORGANIZATION EXTERNAL
        (TYPE ORACLE_LOADER
        DEFAULT DIRECTORY personnel
        ACCESS PARAMETERS

```
        ( RECORDS DELIMITED BY NEWLINE
          FIELDS  TERMINATED  BY  ',')    --change this
depending on ur delimitor
          LOCATION ('emp1.txt') )
          REJECT LIMIT UNLIMITED;

        CREATE TABLE emp_ext2
        ( empcode NUMBER(4), empname VARCHAR2(25),
        job VARCHAR2(25))
         ORGANIZATION EXTERNAL
         ( TYPE ORACLE_LOADER
         DEFAULT DIRECTORY personnel
         ACCESS PARAMETERS
        ( RECORDS DELIMITED BY NEWLINE
         FIELDS TERMINATED BY ',')
         LOCATION ('emp2.txt') )
         REJECT LIMIT UNLIMITED;

spool diff.txt
select empcode||','||empname||','||job
from(select * from emp_ext1
   minus select * from emp_ext2
   union
   select * from emp_ext2
   minus select * from emp_ext1);
spool off;
```

☞ QUESTION **32**

Stored procedures returning column

I have a procedure in a package which should return a column of a table.
The procedure is something like this:

Package body......
Procedure (prefix IN varchar2, names OUT varchar2) as

I want to retrieve names from same table and return.
The names have a where like condition prefix.

1. How can I use the argument prefix in "where names like 'prefix%'.

2. Irrespective of where this procedure is called, I should be able to return the names.

✍ ANSWER

It should return a single varchar2. Do you want the names concatenated to a single string? Then you could do something like this:

```
CREATE OR REPLACE PROCEDURE prc$find_emps(
search_string IN VARCHAR2, names OUT VARCHAR2)
IS
  CURSOR c_emps(c_search VARCHAR2)
    IS
    SELECT MAX(SUBSTR(SYS_CONNECT_BY_PATH(last_
```

```
name,',' ),2)) x
  FROM ( SELECT last_name
        , ROW_NUMBER() OVER (ORDER BY last_name)
curr
        , ROW_NUMBER() OVER (ORDER BY last_name)-1
prev
      FROM employees
      WHERE last_name like c_search
      ORDER BY last_name
    )
  CONNECT BY prev = prior curr
  START WITH curr = 1;
BEGIN
  OPEN c_emps(search_string);
  FETCH c_emps INTO names;
  CLOSE c_emps;
END;
/
sho err

SET SERVEROUT ON

DECLARE
  v_emps VARCHAR2 (4000);
BEGIN
  prc$find_emps('A%', v_emps);
  dbms_output.put_line('Employees with ''A%''');
  dbms_output.put_line(v_emps);
```

```
prc$find_emps('T%', v_emps);
dbms_output.put_line('Employees with ''T%''');
dbms_output.put_line(v_emps);
prc$find_emps('Ma%', v_emps);
dbms_output.put_line('Employees with ''Ma%''');
dbms_output.put_line(v_emps);
END;
/
```

```
DROP PROCEDURE prc$find_emps
/
```
It runs like this:

```
SQL> @C:\useful\orafaq
```

Procedure created.

No errors.
Employees with 'A%'
Abel,Ande,Atkinson,Austin
Employees with 'T%'
Taylor,Taylor,Tobias,Tucker,Tuvault
Employees with 'Ma%'
Mallin,Markle,Marlow,Marvins,Matos,Mavris

PL/SQL procedure successfully completed.

Procedure dropped.

☞ QUESTION **33**

Ref Cursor Return Parameter

I have created a package as follows:

CREATE OR REPLACE PACKAGE Pkg_Req_Users
AS
TYPE curREQUSERS IS REF CURSOR;
PROCEDURE P_CHECK_ADMIN (v_ADMINUSER OUT
Pkg_Req_Users.curREQUSERS);
PROCEDURE   P_CHECK_USER   (v_USERNAME
VARCHAR2,v_REQUSER OUT NUMBER);
end;

CREATE OR REPLACE PACKAGE BODY Pkg_Req_Users
AS
/* This Procedure will check for the Administrator, if valid
then Admin ID will be returned */
PROCEDURE P_CHECK_ADMIN (v_ADMINUSER OUT
Pkg_Req_Users.curREQUSERS)
AS
BEGIN
OPEN v_ADMINUSER FOR
SELECT USER_ID, USER_NAME FROM DPM_MGMT.
USERS WHERE SECURITY_LEVEL IN
(SELECT   SECURITY_LEVEL   FROM   DPM_MGMT.
SECURITY_CLEARANCE WHERE ROLE_MANAGER=1)
AND UPPER (USER_NAME) NOT LIKE '%SYSTEM%'
UNION ALL
SELECT 0,'OTHERS' FROM DUAL
UNION ALL
SELECT -1,' ' FROM DUAL;
END;

/* This Procedure will check for the User, if already present will return 1 else 0 */
```
PROCEDURE       P_CHECK_USER       (v_USERNAME
VARCHAR2,v_REQUSER OUT NUMBER)
AS
v_COUNT NUMBER:=0;
BEGIN
SELECT COUNT (*) INTO v_COUNT FROM DPM_MGMT.
USER_REQUEST_LOG
WHERE  UPPER (REQUEST_USER_NAME)  =  UPPER(v_
USERNAME) AND STATUS='P';
IF v_COUNT>0 THEN
v_REQUSER:=1;
ELSE
v_REQUSER:=0;
END IF;
END;
end;
```

As you can see I am returning ref cursor to the calling env (here its .Net). The package runs fine. Now the problem is after awhile it has produced an error, (too many cursors opened).

How do I rectify this in the procedure so as not to get this error, and return my ref cursor successfully?

✍ ANSWER

It is the responsibility of the calling program (.NET) to close the cursor when it is done fetching from it. Apparently it is not closing the cursor, which is why you are hitting the exception.

There is also the open_cursors parameter (alter system or alter session), Increasing this value may just hide the problem a little longer, not fix it.

There is nothing wrong with your procedure.

☞ QUESTION 34

Difference between Execute and DBMS_SQL

In the procedure I used below, given methods to drop a table, what is the difference between 'execute immediate' and 'DBMS_SQL.PARSE' package? Both are working.

Which is faster in execution?

vsql varchar2(100):='drop user '||v_user_check;
execute immediate vsql;

Or;

cr number:=DBMS_SQL.OPEN_CURSOR;
DBMS_SQL.PARSE(cr, vsql ,DBMS_SQL.V7);

Which command is better to use in PLSQL if I am using oracle9i Re1?

✎ ANSWER

Execute immediate is faster than dbms_sql. This is also documented at:
http://www.lc.leidenuniv.nl/awcourse/oracle/appdev.920/a96590/adg09dyn.htm#26586

Try and verify it by creating a test case as well.

DBMS_SQL predates EXECUTE IMMEDIATE in PL/SQL. DBMS_SQL was all we had in v7. EXECUTE IMMEDIATE is now (since v8.0) the preferred method of dynamic SQL in PL/SQL.

DBMS_SQL is still maintained because of the inability of EXECUTE IMMEDIATE to perform a so-called "Method 4 Dynamic SQL", where the name/number of SELECT columns or the name/number of bind variables is dynamic.

☞ QUESTION 35

Can't see any data

I'm trying to create a member procedure. I want to be able to add data using the following procedure:

```
create or replace type book as object(
name varchar2(20),
member procedure add_book(oracle in varchar2)
);
/

create or replace type body book as
member procedure add_book(oracle in varchar2) is begin
name := oracle;
end;
end;
/

create table book_tab of book;
declare
newbook book := new book('test');
begin
newbook.add_book('oracle');
end;
/
```

Procedure creates successfully, but when I select * from book_tab I don't see my data (test).

Why is this?

✍ ANSWER

You declared a local variable of the type book (newbook). In your declaration you gave it the name 'test'. Afterwards you changed the name to 'oracle' via your add_book member function. That's all you did. You forgot to insert the newly created book into your table.

Try this instead:

```
DECLARE newbook book := new book('test');
BEGIN
  newbook.add_book('oracle');
  INSERT INTO BOOK_TAB
  VALUES (newbook);
END;
/

select * from book_tab;
```

☞ QUESTION 36

Replacing Null Values from existing values in table

Using 9i R(2).
Tbl_1
Col_A varchar2
Col_B varchar2
Col_C varchar3
(no PK/FK)

I want to inset the missing values (null values) of columns B & C by taking values from filled values from same table on base of Col_A.

Examples:

Col_A || Col_B || Col_C
Item_1 || Red || 2Kg
Item_2 || Blue || 1.5 Kg
Item_1 || Null || Null

I want to inset values in the Null value fields of Row3 (Col_B & CoL_C) from Row1 as Col_A at both rows.

How can I do this efficiently?

✍ ANSWER

You can update tbl_1 t1:
    set (col_b, col_c) = (select t2.col_b, t2.col

```
          from tbl_1 t2
          where t2.col_a = t1.col_a
            and t2.col_b is not null
            and t2.col_c is not null
            and rownum = 1)
  where col_b is null
  and col_c is null;
```

The rownum check is only necessary if you ever had a case where there would be multiple rows of a particular col_a value that had NOT NULL values for col_b and col_c.

☞ QUESTION 37

Fetch value from record type using dyn sql

I am getting an error while executing the following block.

```
declare
cursor c1 is select col_name from test_1;
/* Where test_1 is a table having one column (say x datatype
varchar2) with data as "a","b","C" --> 3 rows, means attribute
name of below mentioned Pl/SQL record
(my_record) is stored */
TYPE my_record IS RECORD
(
a varchar2(10),
b varchar2(10),
c varchar2(10)
);
g_my_val my_record;
test varchar2(100);
begin
g_my_val.a := '1234' ;
g_my_val.b := '123' ;
g_my_val.c := '12' ;
for i in c1
loop
execute immediate('select  g_my_val.' ||i.col_name ||' from
dual') into test;
/* Means the query should look like
select g_my_val.a into test from dual ; ---> 1st iteration
select g_my_val.b into test from dual ; ---> 2nd iteration
select g_my_val.c into test from dual ; ---> 3rd iteration
*/
dbms_output.put_line(test || ' record column value');
```

```
/*
Output should be
1234 record column value ---> 1st iteration
123 record column value ---> 2nd iteration
12 record column value ---> 3rd iteration
*/
end loop;
end;
/
```

Error :

```
declare
*
ERROR at line 1:
ORA-00904: "G_MY_VAL"."A": invalid identifier
ORA-06512: at line 19
```

How do I fix this?

✍ ANSWER

You declared your g_my_val in PL/SQL. EXECUTE IMMEDIATE switches to the SQL engine where this variable is not known. The same applies for the TYPE you created in PL/SQL.

☞ QUESTION **38**

pl/sql packages source

Can any db user have access to the other db user pl/sql procedure?

The Problem:

1. User A created the pl/sql package with procedures test1, test2.
2. User B wants to view the source of pl/sql package owned by user A, and also wants to edit those procedures.
3. What are all the privileges user B needs to perform the above actions from user A?

✍ ANSWER

Can any db user have access to the other db user pl/sql procedure? No, except db A, other users do not have access, unless, such access is explicitly given by db A.

For questions 2 and 3:

Such access can be given by the command:

grant all on a.<procedure_name> to b;

(here <procedure_name> is the name of the procedure , on which you want to grant access.)

Remember that, after giving that access, when user B wants to edit the procedure, he has to refer to the procedure as a. <procedure_name> (i.e. the username "A". has to be there)

☞ QUESTION **39**

Writing debug messages into an external (.txt) file using utl_file package

I basically want to write debug messages into an external (.txt) file.
So I am using the utl_file package for that purpose. Here is the procedure I am using to write the debug messages.

```
create or replace procedure debugfile(str varchar2) as
f1 utl_file.file_type;
begin
f1 := utl_file.fopen('\tmp', 'debug.txt', 'W');
utl_file.put_line(f1, string);
utl_file.fclose(f1);
end;
```

And here is the sample code where I am calling this procedure.

```
declare
a number;
b number;
c number;
begin
a := 10;
debugfile('a = '||a); --calling the debugfile procedure to wirte
the debug message.
b := 20;
debugfile('b = '||b); --calling the debugfile procedure to wirte
the debug message.
c := a + b;
```

debugfile('c = 'IIc); --calling the debugfile procedure to wirte the debug message.
end;

What's happening is that only the last message is being written into the file.
That is because every time the procedure is being called, the file gets rewritten and the previous messages are getting overwritten.

How do I get all of the 3 messages in the above piece of code into a single file?
I may have hundreds of messages in my code. How do I write all of them into a single file?

✍ ANSWER

Check your procedure.

```
create or replace procedure debugfile(str varchar2) as
f1 utl_file.file_type;
begin
f1 := utl_file.fopen('\tmp', 'debug.txt', 'W');
utl_file.put_line(f1, string);
utl_file.fclose(f1);
end;
```

See it? You are already closing the file. When you try to write another line, you start again at the first line of the file so the last string is overwritten.

☞ QUESTION 40

pl/sql tables

I have this procedure where I use temporary tables to insert the results of a comparison. Inside the procedure, to create the table, I use the "execute immediate command". At the end of the procedure, I select from this temporary table.

It gives the error: table not found. I was told it is because using execute immediate, the command is taken as a text.

As an alternative I used pl/sql tables, and the same problem occured. When I went to select from the table it did not find it, as pl/sql tables do not physically exist. In navigating the net, I discovered that select does not work with pl/sql tables. Instead all net references I found used dbms_output. put_line.

I need to retrieve all table contents in a select so I can call the procedure from crystal reports.

✍ ANSWER

Don't use temporary tables, pl/sql tables or separate inserts and so forth. Just open a ref cursor for one big select statement, assuming that Crystal Reports will accept a ref cursor.

☞ QUESTION 41

See data from a table dynamically

I would like to see the values from the table using pure pl/
SQL.
That is, the input parameters will the table_name.
All the column values from that table should be displayed,
irrespective of column numbers, column data type, etc.

The main problem will be to declare the variable (type) to
store the table data dynamically.

I also tried to take a look at REF CURSORS, but the problem
is I could not create a variable type to COLLECT the refcursor.
The number of columns and type of columns varies. It's
purely depending on Input table name.

How do I get the result in pure PL/SQL way?

How do I fix the error?

✍ ANSWER

There is one way of doing this:

VAR thecur REFCURSOR
VAR tablename VARCHAR2(30);

EXEC :tablename := 'EMPLOYEES';

```
BEGIN
  OPEN :thecur FOR 'SELECT * FROM '|| :tablename||'
WHERE ROWNUM < 2';
END;
/
```

PRINT :thecur;

```
EXEC :tablename := 'JOBS';
BEGIN
  OPEN :thecur FOR 'SELECT * FROM '|| :tablename||'
WHERE ROWNUM < 2';
END;
/
```

PRINT :thecur;

If you run it as a script, you get this:

SQL> @C:\useful\orafaq

PL/SQL procedure successfully completed.

PL/SQL procedure successfully completed.

EMPLOYEE_ID FIRST_NAME   LAST_NAME

---------- ----------------- ---------------------

EMAIL   PHONE_NUMBER   HIRE_DATE
JOB_ID   SALARY

---------------------- ------------------ -------- --------- ---------
COMMISSION_PCT MANAGER_ID DEPARTMENT_ID
------------- --------- -------------
    100 Steven   King
SKING   515.123.4567   17-JUN-87 AD_PRES   24000
                     90

PL/SQL procedure successfully completed.

PL/SQL procedure successfully completed.

JOB_ID   JOB_TITLE   MIN_SALARY MAX_SALARY
--------- ------------------------------- --------- ----------
AD_PRES   President   20000   40000

☞ QUESTION **42**

SQL*Plus not responding to UTL_REF package

When I execute any procedure from UTL_REF package in SQL*Plus, I don't get any response. Everything blocks, and I can only get out with CTRL+ALT+DEL.

I have the execute privilege on package UTL_REF, as shown below:

SQL> select object_name, object type from all_objects where object_name='UTL_REF';

OBJECT_NAME   OBJECT_TYPE
---------------------------- ------------------
UTL_REF   PACKAGE
UTL_REF   PACKAGE BODY
UTL_REF   SYNONYM

I'm trying to execute the following block:

```
declare
 ref REF clConsum;
 ob  clConsum;
begin
    select  REF(a)  into  ref  from  tabConsum  a  where
a.nrOp=96;
 utl_ref.select_object(ref,ob);
end;
```

When utl_ref.select_object(refBon,obBon); is missing, the block is successfully executed, but with that line of code,

SQL*Plus is not responding.
If I replace that line with a corresponding query, like beow, the block is successfully executed:

```
declare
  ref REF clConsum;
  ob  clConsum;
begin
    select REF(a) into ref from tabConsum a where
a.nrOp=96;
    select value(a) into ob from tabConsum a where
ref(a)=ref;
end;
```

I'm using the following versions:

SQL> SELECT banner FROM v$version;

BANNER

Oracle9i Enterprise Edition Release 9.0.1.3.1 - Production
PL/SQL Release 9.0.1.3.1 - Production
CORE   9.0.1.2.0   Production
TNS for 32-bit Windows: Version 9.0.1.3.0 - Production
NLSRTL Version 9.0.1.3.0 - Production

✍ ANSWER

If I waited long enough, approximately 4 minutes, I would get an ORA-00600 error.

I tried installing a different version of Oracle Database and since then its now working.

☞ QUESTION 43

Generating a number for a name

I am using html to input the data in the table master_network. Say I input a network_name (e.g David) and if the name does not exist in the master_network, the case_study_number should be 0. If it existed, then the case_study_number would be one more than the last case_study_number for that network_name. How do I input the date on the server automatically if that network_name was entered?

For example, if the network_name does not exist the table should look like:

NETWORK_NAME	CASE_STUDY_NUMBER	NETWORK_CODE	NETWORK_DESCRIPTION	STUDY_DATE
DARRELL	0	firsttest	first example	23-FEB-06
DAVID	0	base	testing	13-FEB-06
DAVID	1	loadflow	load test	14-FEB-06
DAVID	2	powerflow	power test	20-FEB-06

And if the network_name does exist the table should look like:

NETWORK_NAME	CASE_STUDY_NUMBER	NETWORK_CODE	NETWORK_DESCRIPTION	STUDY_DATE
DARRELL	0	firsttest	first example	23-FEB-06
DARRELL	1	secondtest	second example	24-FEB-06
DARRELL	2	thirdtest	third example	25-FEB-06
DAVID	0	base	testing	13-FEB-06
DAVID	1	loadflow	load test	14-FEB-06
DAVID	2	powerflow	power test	20-FEB-06

This is the master_network table:

CREATE TABLE master_network(
network_name   VARCHAR2(20),
case_study_number   NUMBER(2),
network_code   VARCHAR2(20),
network_description VARCHAR2 (100),
study_date   DATE,
PRIMARY KEY(case_study_number,network_code));

When the information is placed in master_network table, then the case_study_number and network_code automatically goes in the line_data table:

CREATE TABLE Line_data(
case_study_number   NUMBER(2),
network_code VARCHAR2(20),
from_bus   NUMBER(5),
to_bus   NUMBER(5),
resistance   NUMBER(4,2),
reactance   NUMBER(4,2),
CONSTRAINT   FK_MASTERBUSTYPES   FOREIGN
KEY(case_study_number, network_code)
REFERENCES   master_network(case_study_number,
network_code)

✎ ANSWER

You can create a trigger on the master table (before insert trigger), which checks for the master table's row contents, and accordingly inserts the data into the master table, as per your requirement. It also populates record into the table Line_data as well.

☞ QUESTION 44

Stored Procedure

Is there any way or any tools like TOAD to interpret /trace the execution of a procedure line by line?

✍ ANSWER

Yes, there's Free tool, provided by Oracle Corp. called SQL Developer (formerly known as Project Raptor) and can be downloaded from the provided page.

☞ QUESTION 45

To load few columns from Excel sheet to Oracle table

I have an Excel file and I want to load only a few columns from excel to oracle.

How can I do this?

✍ ANSWER

One possible way would be this: in Excel, use "Save As ..." and save data as a CSV file. Use SQL*Loader and load data into Oracle table.

You can also try using OLE2 Package. By using this, you can read/write on a specific cell from/to a excel sheet.

☞ QUESTION 46

Execution Time Problem of a stored procedure

I've written a stored procedure which will be sorting a table having 35 lakh records. But a lot of business logic is involved that needs a lot of sorts, i.e GROUP by and ORDER clauses. My question is what should be the ideal size for sort_area_ size, and my TEMP tablespace.

The problem is that I can create a concatinated index on the columns, which I am referring in the WHERE clause. It is showing a very good performance. The problem is that, on the Production database Server, which is in the US, is not willing to create that Index. The procedure is taking 5hrs to get executed and if I create that index, it gets executed within 15 minutes.

What can I do to improve performance of the stored procedure without creating a index?

Here is the sample code of that procedure.

CREATE OR REPLACE PROCEDURE SP_CUSTACCT_ZIP_ LEGAL__ENTITY
AS
CURSOR mycus IS SELECT DISTINCT ZIP_5_CD FROM cust_acct; -- main qry get the distinct 5 digit codes
v_zipcode VARCHAR2(20);
ROWS NUMBER:=0;
ddl VARCHAR2(20);
usr VARCHAR2(20);

```
BEGIN
dbms_output.put_line('Please Wait Few Minutes ....');
ddl:='truncate table topn';
EXECUTE IMMEDIATE (ddl);
dbms_output.put_line('** Table Truncated **');
SELECT USER INTO usr FROM dual;
FOR j IN mycus LOOP
v_zipcode:=j.ZIP_5_CD;
DECLARE
maxcnt NUMBER; -- nof rows having with same max(cnt)
maxsls NUMBER; -- when we dealing with sum(AVG_
THREE_MTH_NET_SLS_VOL)
nr NUMBER; -- means nofrows whose count(*)=max(cnt)
sr NUMBER; -- means sales rows i.e noofrows whose
count(*)=max(sls)
BEGIN
SELECT MAX(c) INTO maxcnt FROM (SELECT /*+
cache(cust_acct)*/ COUNT(*) c FROM cust_acct WHERE
ZIP_5_CD=v_zipcode GROUP BY ZIP_5_CD,legal_ent);
SELECT COUNT(*) INTO nr FROM (SELECT /*+ cache(cust_
acct)*/ ZIP_5_CD,legal_ent,COUNT(*),SUM(AVG_THREE_
MTH_NET_SLS_VOL) FROM cust_acct WHERE ZIP_5_
CD=v_zipcode GROUP BY ZIP_5_CD,legal_ent
HAVING COUNT(*)=(SELECT MAX(c) FROM (SELECT /*+
cache(cust_acct)*/ COUNT(*) c FROM cust_acct WHERE
ZIP_5_CD=v_zipcode GROUP BY ZIP_5_CD,legal_ent) )) ;
IF (nr>1) THEN -- then get all those recs and this time
consider sum(AVG_THREE_MTH_NET_SLS_VOL)
-- get the max(sls)
SELECT MAX(sls) INTO maxsls FROM (SELECT /*+
cache(cust_acct)*/    SUM(AVG_THREE_MTH_NET_SLS_
VOL) sls FROM cust_acct WHERE ZIP_5_CD=v_zipcode
GROUP BY ZIP_5_CD,legal_ent
HAVING COUNT(*)=(SELECT MAX(c) FROM (SELECT /*+
cache(cust_acct)*/ COUNT(*) c FROM cust_acct WHERE
```

ZIP_5_CD=v_zipcode GROUP BY ZIP_5_CD,legal_ent)));
SELECT COUNT(*) INTO sr FROM (SELECT /*+ cache(cust_
acct)*/ ZIP_5_CD,legal_ent,COUNT(*),SUM(AVG_THREE_
MTH_NET_SLS_VOL) FROM cust_acct WHERE ZIP_5_
CD=v_zipcode GROUP BY ZIP_5_CD,legal_ent
HAVING   SUM(AVG_THREE_MTH_NET_SLS_
VOL)=(SELECT MAX(c) FROM (SELECT SUM(AVG_
THREE_MTH_NET_SLS_VOL) c FROM cust_acct WHERE
ZIP_5_CD=v_zipcode GROUP BY ZIP_5_CD,legal_ent))) ;
-- usefull for else part
IF (sr=1) THEN
DECLARE
CURSOR   sr_only_1   IS   SELECT   ZIP_5_CD,legal_
ent,COUNT(*) c,SUM(AVG_THREE_MTH_NET_SLS_VOL)
sls FROM cust_acct WHERE ZIP_5_CD=v_zipcode GROUP
BY ZIP_5_CD,legal_ent HAVING SUM(AVG_THREE_MTH_
NET_SLS_VOL)=
(SELECT MAX(sls) FROM (SELECT /*+ cache(cust_acct)*/
SUM(AVG_THREE_MTH_NET_SLS_VOL) sls FROM cust_
acct WHERE ZIP_5_CD=v_zipcode GROUP BY ZIP_5_
CD,legal_ent HAVING COUNT(*)=(SELECT MAX(c) FROM
(SELECT COUNT(*) c FROM cust_acct WHERE ZIP_5_
CD=v_zipcode GROUP BY ZIP_5_CD,legal_ent)))));
BEGIN
FOR i IN sr_only_1 LOOP
INSERT INTO ZIP_LEGAL_ENTITY VALUES(i.zip_5_cd,i.
legal_ent,SYSDATE,usr);
COMMIT;
END LOOP;
END;
ELSE -- that is more no. of rows with max (sls), then arrange
all those recs order by legal entity and display and insert
DECLARE
CURSOR sr_more IS SELECT * FROM (SELECT ROWNUM
rno,tmp.* FROM (SELECT /*+ cache(cust_acct)*/ ZIP_5_

```
CD,legal_ent,COUNT(*)    c,SUM(AVG_THREE_MTH_NET_
SLS_VOL)  sls  FROM  cust_acct  WHERE  ZIP_5_CD=v_
zipcode
GROUP BY ZIP_5_CD,legal_ent HAVING SUM(AVG_THREE_
MTH_NET_SLS_VOL)=(SELECT MAX(sls) FROM (SELECT
SUM(AVG_THREE_MTH_NET_SLS_VOL) sls FROM cust_
acct WHERE ZIP_5_CD=v_zipcode GROUP BY
ZIP_5_CD,legal_ent HAVING COUNT(*)=(SELECT MAX(c)
FROM  (SELECT  COUNT(*)  c  FROM  cust_acct  WHERE
ZIP_5_CD=v_zipcode  GROUP  BY  ZIP_5_CD,legal_ent) )))
ORDER BY legal_ent) tmp) WHERE rno=1;
BEGIN
FOR i IN sr_more LOOP
INSERT  INTO  ZIP_LEGAL_ENTITY  VALUES(i.zip_5_cd,i.
legal_ent,SYSDATE,usr);
COMMIT;
END LOOP;
END;
END IF; -- eof inner if
ELSE -- i.e nr=1 then simply display only 1 rec
DECLARE
CURSOR    nr_only_1    IS    SELECT    ZIP_5_CD,legal_
ent,COUNT(*)  c,SUM(AVG_THREE_MTH_NET_SLS_VOL)
sls FROM cust_acct WHERE ZIP_5_CD=v_zipcode GROUP
BY ZIP_5_CD,legal_ent
HAVING COUNT(*)=(SELECT MAX(c) FROM (SELECT /*+
cache(cust_acct)*/  COUNT(*)  c  FROM  cust_acct  WHERE
ZIP_5_CD=v_zipcode GROUP BY ZIP_5_CD,legal_ent) );
BEGIN
FOR i IN nr_only_1 LOOP
INSERT  INTO  ZIP_LEGAL_ENTITY  VALUES(i.zip_5_cd,i.
legal_ent,SYSDATE,usr);
COMMIT;
END LOOP;
END;
```

END IF; -- outer if
END; -- eof inner block
END LOOP; –eof main loop
EXCEPTION
WHEN OTHERS THEN – if any errors simply rollback
ROLLBACK;
dbms_output.put_line('*****   ERROR   ENCOUNTERED ******');
dbms_output.put_line('Error Code :'||SQLCODE);
dbms_output.put_line('Error Occured :'||SQLERRM);
END; -- eof main block
/

✍ ANSWER

If an index is all it takes to solve the problem, then they are just being stubborn and silly. You can give them their choice of index or slow execution, and if they complain about the execution time, remind them that all it would take to fix it is an index, and they made the choice.

However, it looks like your code could be greatly simplified. You might be able to achieve significant improvement and make use of whatever indexes may or may not already exist. You should eliminate unnecessary variables and queries. Dbms_output won't display until the end, so there is no point in providing a message advising to wait. Instead of using hints, you should analyze using dbms_stats to gather statistics to allow the cost-based optimizer to choose the best execution plan. Don't commit within a loop. Better yet, don't loop, just "insert into ... select ...". Instead of counting the number of rows and storing that to a variable and using an if statement to check it, and having one insert that inserts one row if there is only one, and another insert that inserts only the first ordered row if there are multiple rows. Just use the one insert to insert the first row.

It looks like your whole procedure can probably be simplified to something like what I have shown below. It is not tested, due to a lack of tables and data to test with. I did not check all of the logical thoroughly, but it should be enough to give you the general idea. It could probably be simplified even further.

```
CREATE OR REPLACE PROCEDURE sp_custact_zip_legal_
_entity
AS
BEGIN
  EXECUTE IMMEDIATE ('TRUNCATE table topn');
  FOR j IN
   (SELECT DISTINCT zip_5_cd FROM cust_acct)
  LOOP
   INSERT INTO zip_legal_entity
   SELECT zip_5_cd, legal_ent, SYSDATE, USER
   FROM   (SELECT zip_5_cd, legal_ent
        FROM   cust_acct
        WHERE  zip_5_cd = j.zip_5_cd
        GROUP  BY zip_5_cd, legal_ent
        HAVING SUM (avg_three_mth_net_sls_vol) =
           (SELECT MAX (sls)
       FROM   (SELECT SUM (avg_three_mth_net_sls_vol) sls
              FROM   cust_acct
              WHERE  zip_5_cd = j.zip_5_cd
              GROUP  BY zip_5_cd, legal_ent
           HAVING COUNT (*) =
              (SELECT MAX (c)
              FROM   (SELECT COUNT (*) c
              FROM   cust_acct
                 WHERE  zip_5_cd = j.zip_5_cd
```

```
                    GROUP  BY zip_5_cd, legal_ent))))
        ORDER BY legal_ent)
    WHERE ROWNUM = 1;
  END LOOP;
    COMMIT; -- may want to do this outside the procedure
instead
EXCEPTION
  WHEN OTHERS THEN
    ROLLBACK;
    RAISE;
END sp_custact_zip_legal_entity;
/
.
```

☞ QUESTION 47

Decoding

I am executing this in toad and I keep getting the ORA-01460: "unimplemented or unreasonable conversion requested".

Here is the statement:

SELECT   decode(:pExt,'',decode(:pName,'','',:pName),:
pExt||decode(:pName,'','',',') || :pName)
FROM Dual;

Both pExt and pName are strings and passed as null. If I give values to even one of them then I do not get an error. Only when both are passed as null do I get an error.

When I execute this as a part of a procedure, I do not get any error. Null or not null.

Why does this occur?

How can this issue be resolved?

✍ ANSWER

Be careful with your use of ''null', and don't expect them to always behave interchangeably. If you mean something to be null, use the keyword null.

For example:

MYDBA > create table t1(a varchar2(30));

Table created.

MYDBA > insert into t1 values ('');

1 row created.

MYDBA > select count(*) from t1 where a is null;

  COUNT(*)

      1

MYDBA > select count(*) from t1 where a = '';

  COUNT(*)

      0

MYDBA >

And see if this logic helps in what I think you are trying to do:

MYDBA > create table t1 (id number, a varchar2(10), b varchar2(10));

Table created.

MYDBA > insert into t1 values (1, 'a', 'b');

1 row created.

MYDBA > insert into t1 values (2, 'a', null);

1 row created.

MYDBA > insert into t1 values (3, null, 'b');

1 row created.

MYDBA > insert into t1 values (4, null, null);

1 row created.

MYDBA > commit;

Commit complete.

MYDBA > select id, a, b from t1;

```
    ID A        B
--------- --------- ---------
     1 a        b
     2 a
     3        b
     4
```

MYDBA > select id, a || ',' || b from t1;

```
    ID A||','||B
--------- --------------------
     1 a,b
     2 a,
     3 ,b
     4 ,
```

MYDBA > select id, a || b from t1;

```
    ID A||B
```

```
-----------------------------
    1 ab
    2 a
    3 b
    4
```

MYDBA > select id, trim(both ',' from a || ',' || b) from t1;

```
    ID TRIM(BOTH',',FROMA||',
--------- --------------------
    1 a,b
    2 a
    3 b
    4
```

MYDBA > select id, decode(a,null,b,decode(b,null,a,a||',||b)) from t1;

```
    ID DECODE(A,NULL,B,DECOD
--------- --------------------
    1 a,b
    2 a
    3 b
    4
```
MYDBA > select id, nvl2(a,a||nvl2(b,',||b,null),b) from t1;

```
    ID NVL2(A,A||NVL2(B,',|
--------- --------------------
    1 a,b
    2 a
    3 b
    4
```

MYDBA >

☞ QUESTION 48

Use of one or two triggers

My requirement is to have a single table. For example:

SQL> select * from token;

SNO VALUE

-------- ------------------------

   1 abc*def*xyz*jhn*mnb*zaq

Now in this table, there are 2 kinds of data:

1) data where value column has 5 stars

2) and data where value column has 4 stars

My task is:

*)seperate the data with 5 stars, and everytime an insertion is done in token table, insert it into token1 table in such a way that in token1, there are 6 columns.

Column1 should have abc, column2 should have def, etc.

*) seperate the data with 4 stars and everytime an insertion is done in token table, insert into token2 table (with the same pattern). For instance, if token 1 data is:

gautam*ajay*chandu*vijay*rahul

token2 column1 should have gautam, column2 should have ajay, and so on..

I used an improved trigger, which will get the data which has
* in it, and insert into another table in the above mentioned
pattern.

```
create or replace trigger trig_valchange after insert on tbl_
field_valchange
declare
cursor mycrs is select field_newvalue from tbl_field_
valchange where field_newvalue like '%*%';
v_vals tbl_field_valchange.field_newvalue%type;
v_errorcode number;
v_errortext varchar2(300);
begin
delete from tbl_modemstatistics;
open mycrs;
loop
fetch mycrs into v_vals;
exit when mycrs%notfound;
  insert into tbl_modemstatistics(min_ebno,avg_ebno,max_
  txpower,avg_txpower,modem_date,modem_time)
  values(substr(v_vals,1,instr(v_vals,'*')-1),
        substr(v_vals,instr(v_vals,'*')+1,instr(v_vals,'*',1,2)-1-
instr(v_vals,'*')),
        substr(v_vals,instr(v_vals,'*',1,2)+1,instr(v_vals,'*',1,3)-
1-instr(v_vals,'*',1,2)),
        substr(v_vals,instr(v_vals,'*',1,3)+1,instr(v_vals,'*',1,4)-
1-instr(v_vals,'*',1,3)),
        substr(v_vals,instr(v_vals,'*',1,4)+1,instr(v_vals,'*',1,5)-
1-instr(v_vals,'*',1,4)),
    substr(v_vals,instr(v_vals,'*',1,5)+1));
  end loop;
  close mycrs;
exception
  when no_data_found then
  dbms_output.put_line('there is no data');
```

```
when others then
v_errorcode:=sqlcode;
v_errortext:=sqlerrm;
  dbms_output.put_line('Error code is '||v_errorcode||' and
message is ' ||v_errortext);
 end;
```

Now I need to filter out the data with 5 stars, and 4 stars, and insert them into the appropriate tables.

I know a query which gets me the count of number of occurrences of * in the column. The query is:

```
SELECT (LENGTH (value) - NVL (LENGTH (REPLACE
(value,'*','')),0))/LENGTH('*') "Count"
FROM token
```

How do I make use of this? Should I filter it out in the beginning cursor statement itself, and use two triggers?

Is it possible to use this query in the loop section of the cursor, and then insert separately? Is it possible this way?

✍ ANSWER

Make use of 2 triggers and in the cursor itself use filtering, whether data should have 4 stars or 5 stars. Do this so that even if both these fire, there will be no problem.

You can also use the 4th parameter of instruction function to make the trigger more easily, and with less code.

☞ QUESTION **49**

ORA 12839 cannot modify an object in parallel after modifying it

I just had a procedure fail with ORA-12839:

"cannot modify an object in parallel after modifying it at 21/12/2005 01:35:24";

At the beginning of the procedure it says 'alter session enable parallel dml', and then does a number of truncates and inserts.

Do these run in turn or does it happen all at the same time?

Could my problem be that there's no commit, after the truncate? Maybe an insert has one session and the truncate still has another locked.

If the Truncate has an implied commit, and that's not the problem, then the problem may be that this procedure does several inserts into a table and does not do a 'Commit' between them.

It appears a 'Transaction' is considered to be up to the next commit or rollback. Is it possible these inserts are affecting or clashing with each other?

✍ ANSWER

I'd have to do a test case to be positive, but my best guess is that yes, it is due to a lack of commit. You can modify the data in parallel with the insert, but truncate is a ddl operation. You would need to commit the parallel insert before issuing any ddl, such as a truncate.

Also, it isn't that parallel means do all of the operations at the same time. Rather, each operation, such as each individual insert statement, would itself internally use parallel processes to complete.

Yes, a commit or rollback defines a transaction by ending it. So be careful of just throwing them in there, because a transaction is a business rule sort of thing.

You may also want to consider not doing the statements using parallel dml.

☞ QUESTION **50**

Trigger is used, data output not coming as desired

I have a table like this, and the name is "token".

token

sno number(5)

value varchar2(300)

My requirement is: now, and for the column value, the data will be something like this.

Gautam*Trilok*Rahul

Ajay*Rahul*Trilok

Trilok*Sachin

Now, i have to create another table, and everytime there is an insertion in the token table, my new table (token1) should have data like this:

token 1

value1 value2 value3

Gautam Trilok Rahul

Ajay Rahul Trilok

Trilok Sachin

I was asked to find the records having 'Trilok', and then seperate, and insert the names seperately into the new table columns.

I used a trigger, as follows:

```
create or replace trigger trig_inmacs1 after insert on token
 declare
cursor mycrs is select value from token where value like
'%Tr%';
v_vals token.value%type;
 v_errorcode number;
 v_errortext varchar2(300);
begin
  delete from token1;
   open mycrs;

 loop
 fetch mycrs into v_vals;
 exit when mycrs%notfound;

        insert   into   token1(value1,value2)   values(substr(v_
vals,1,7),substr(v_vals,9,6));

    end loop;

   close mycrs;

exception
   when no_data_found then
   dbms_output.put_line('there is no data');
   when others then
   v_errorcode:=sqlcode;
   v_errortext:=sqlerrm;
```

dbms_output.put_line('Error code is '||v_errorcode||' and message is ' ||v_errortext);

  end;

Obviously, when I insert into token, the token1 values are somewhat like:

VALUE1 VALUE2

--------- ------

Ajay*Tr lok
Sachin* rilok
Chandu* rilok
Sanjay* rilok
Chandu* rilok
Chandj* rilok
Ravi*Tr lok
Rahul*T ilok
Gautam* rilok*

I need to see to it that the * doesnt appear, and I can seperate the names properly and insert it into the target table's corresponding columns. I know instr has to be used, but somehow I m not getting it.

✍ ANSWER

Try to do this in steps:
In sqlplus see what instr does:

SQL> select instr('Gautam*Trilok*Rahul', '*')
  2 from dual
  3 /

INSTR('GAUTAM*TRILOK*RAHUL','*')

7

On position 7 an asterisk is found.
Now let's play with substr and instr together:

SQL> select substr('Gautam*Trilok*Rahul', 1, instr('Gautam
*Trilok*Rahul', '*'))
  2 from   dual;

SUBSTR(

Gautam*

This appears to be one position too many, so for the first
part, we obviously need
substr(<<string>>, 1, instr(<<string>>, '*') - 1)

Let's search for the next asterisk. For this we use a third
parameter of the instr-function, indicating the starting-
position from where the search must be done.

SQL> select instr('Gautam*Trilok*Rahul', '*', 7 + 1)
  2 from   dual
  3 /

INSTR('GAUTAM*TRILOK*RAHUL','*',7+1)

14

The length of this word is the position of the second asterisk
(minus 1) minus the position of the previous asterisk:

SQL> select substr('Gautam*Trilok*Rahul'

2   , instr('Gautam*Trilok*Rahul', '*', 7) + 1 -- 1 position further than the asterisk

3   , instr('Gautam*Trilok*Rahul', '*', 7 + 1) - 1 - instr ('Gautam*Trilok*Rahul', '*', 7)

4   )

5 from   dual

6 /

SUBSTR

Trilok

So, go and play with it in sqlplus. Get a feeling of how it works and test it in small bits.

☞ QUESTION 51

Initialize populated row type variable

How would I initialize properly, a variable declared as v1 table1% type?

This is populated like:

v1.col1:= 'Col 1 value';
v1.col2:= 'Col 2 value';
v1.col3:= 'Col 3 value';
v1.col4:= 'Col 4 value';
...
vn.coln:= 'Col n value';

Now I want to initialize v1 again. How do I do it?

✍ ANSWER

Just assign NULL to it:

```
Sql>declare
 2   v_emp emp%rowtype;
 3   begin
 4   v_emp.empno := 123;
 5   v_emp.ename := 'John';
 6   dbms_output.put_line ('Name: ' || v_emp.ename );
 7   v_emp := null;
 8   dbms_output.put_line( 'Name: ' || v_emp.ename );
 9 end;
```

An alternative approach is to re-initialize a table-type, you can use .delete:

```
SQL> declare
  2    type rec is record (id number
  3                   , text varchar2 (10)
  4                   );
  5    type tab is table of rec index by binary_integer;
  6    l_tab   tab;
  7    begin
  8    l_tab(1).id := 10;
  9    l_tab(1).text := 'Hello';
 10    l_tab(2).text := 'world';
 11    dbms_output.put_line(l_tab(2).text);
 12    l_tab.delete;
 13    dbms_output.put_line(l_tab(2).text);
 14    end;
 15 /
World
Declare
*
ERROR at line 1:
ORA-01403: no data found
ORA-06512: at line 13
```

☞ QUESTION 52

Cursor taking a lot of time

I have a table with approximately 40 million records. The table looks like this below:

mem_id, eff_date
100, 01/01/2001
100, 02/01/2001
200, 03/01/2003
200, 07/01/2003
200, 03/01/2004

I need to create a new table, using the above table as input, and calculate a column field, term_date. The new table should look as follows:

mem_id, eff_date,term_date
100, 01/01/2001, calculated
100, 02/01/2001, calculated
200, 03/01/2003, calculated
200, 07/01/2003, calculated
200, 03/01/2004, calculated

The calculation logic for term_date uses the eff_date of the next record, if the current record mem_id = next record mem_id. For eg, for mem_id 100 above term date of the first record, is calculated using eff_date of second record.

Since this pretty much involves looping through records, I could only implement it using cursors. However cursors are taking a lot of time I ran a test for 1 million records and it took a day.

Is there an alternative way to implement this to make it run faster?

✍ ANSWER

This can be done in pure SQL using the LEAD analytical function. However, instead of creating another table to do the function, why not just a view of the existing table?

Or an alternative analytic solution would look something like this:

Create table newtab as
Selectmem_id, eff_date, lag(eff_date,1) over (partition by mem_id order by mem_id, eff_date) term_date from oldtab;

☞ QUESTION 53

Nested Record

I did the following procedure:

```
Declare
type emp_1_rec is record(v_name varchar2(30));
type emp_2_rec is record(name emp_1_rec);
name_tab emp_2_rec;
cursor c1 is select ename from test1;
begin
open c1;
loop
fetch c1 into name_tab;
exit when c1%notfound;
dbms_output.put_line(name_tab.name.v_name);
end loop;
end;
```

It ends up in: "Error: ORA-06550: line 0, column 0: PLS-00801: internal error [0]";

But if I run the following code:

```
SQL> declare
  2  type emp_1_rec is record(v_name varchar2(30));
  3  type emp_2_rec is record(name emp_1_rec);
  4  name_tab emp_2_rec;
  5  --cursor c1 is select ename from test1;
  6  begin
  7  name_tab.name.v_name:='scott' ;
  8  dbms_output.put_line(name_tab.name.v_name);
  9  end;
```

```
 10 /
scott
```

PL/SQL procedure successfully completed.

What am I doing wrong in the first procedure?

What can I do to fix it?

✍ ANSWER

You are trying to assign a VARCHAR2 column to a locally declared type. I could easily reproduce it.

```
SQL> declare
  2  type emp_1_rec is record(v_name varchar2(30));
  3  type emp_2_rec is record(name emp_1_rec);
  4  name_tab emp_2_rec;
  5  cursor c1 is select last_name from employees;
  6  begin
  7  open c1;
  8  loop
  9  fetch c1 into name_tab;
 10  exit when c1%notfound;
 11  dbms_output.put_line(name_tab.name.v_name);
 12  end loop;
 13  end;
 14  /
declare
*
ERROR at line 1:
ORA-06550: line 0, column 0:
PLS-00801: internal error [pdticv:CHR/AFC->]
```

If you explicitly store it in the VARCHAR2 member of your type, all will work well. Pay attention to line 9.

```
SQL> declare
  2  type emp_1_rec is record(v_name varchar2(30));
  3  type emp_2_rec is record(name emp_1_rec);
  4  name_tab emp_2_rec;
  5  cursor c1 is select last_name from employees;
  6  begin
  7  open c1;
  8  loop
  9  fetch c1 into name_tab.name;
 10  exit when c1%notfound;
 11  dbms_output.put_line(name_tab.name.v_name);
 12  end loop;
 13  end;
 14  /
King
Kochhar
De Haan
<<...snip...>>
Higgins
Gietz
```

PL/SQL procedure successfully completed. The lesson is to make sure both sides of an assignment are of the same type.

☞ QUESTION 54

Eliminating duplicate rows while using SQL loader

I am using SQL Loader to insert records from a flat file onto a table. Some of the records in my flat file are duplicates and I need to insert only the first encountered one. The records in the flat file are sorted.

Is there any way I can insert only the first row encountered?

✎ ANSWER

Refer restrict duplicate data through SQL*loader [message #144909].

Essentially do the following:

a) Use unique constraint and let sqlldr reject records. The danger being that you need to check to ensure no other records are also rejected;

Or

b) Load into stage table, and use SQL to insert unique records to main tables. I always try to use this approach unless doing a quick and dirty load. For production loads, I usually make the stage tables all varchar2, (4000) or similar, so nothing fails, unless the data is really corrupt. I then do validation in subsequent load. This way, errors can be generated to a stage error table and reported nicely to users' simplifying the data.

An alternative approach will be to create a unique index on the columns, and then the duplicates will just fail. Note that every duplicate will write a line to the log, as well as to the BAD file, so it is not really "silent". This won't work for direct-path loads.

You could also use an Externally Organized Table (Google it), and then eliminate duplicates with a SQL statement as you insert into the target table.

☞ QUESTION 55

Date format for a column in External Tables

I have a flat file with a field of data-type DATE, in the format DDMMYYYY.
I created an external table to load the data from this flat file to oracle database.
My question is, do I have to specify the date format while creating the external table?

If so, where do I specify the date format and how?

✍ ANSWER

You can follow from the contents of c:\oralce\test.dat:

30012006,
29012006,
31012006,

scott@ORA92> CREATE OR REPLACE DIRECTORY my_dir AS 'c:\oracle'
 2 /

Directory created.

scott@ORA92> CREATE TABLE test_tab
 2   (date_col DATE)
 3   ORGANIZATION EXTERNAL
 4   (TYPE ORACLE_LOADER
 5   DEFAULT DIRECTORY my_dir
 6   ACCESS PARAMETERS

```
7          (FIELDS TERMINATED BY ","
8              (DATE_COL CHAR (255) DATE_FORMAT DATE
MASK "ddmmyyyy"))
9          LOCATION ('test.dat'))
10 /
```

Table created.

```
scott@ORA92> SELECT * FROM test_tab
 2 /
```

DATE_COL

30-JAN-06
29-JAN-06
31-JAN-06

☞ QUESTION 56

Repeating Group Removal

I have a column with repeating value which I want to fix as follows:

Tbl_A
Col_1
225
221,222
41-45, 49
332-337, 211, 63-66

Where (41-45) means 41, 42, 43, 44, 45, etc.
& (221,222) means 221 and 222
332-337, 211, 63-66 means both above;

I want to overcome these repeating values by adding the separate rows (with same values of other columns) for each value.

How can I build a procedure and function for it which can be understood?

✍ ANSWER

Do as follows:

scott@ORA92> SELECT col_1 FROM tbl_a
  2 /

COL_1

225
221,222
41-45, 49
332-337, 211, 63-66

```
scott@ORA92> CREATE OR REPLACE PROCEDURE
remove_groups
  2  AS
  3    v_val    VARCHAR2(32767);
  4    v_first  VARCHAR2(32767);
  5    v_last   VARCHAR2(32767);
  6  BEGIN
  7    FOR r IN
  8       (SELECT col_1 || ',' AS val,
  9              (LENGTH (col_1)
 10                - LENGTH (REPLACE (col_1, ',', '')))
 11                + 1 AS num
 12        FROM       tbl_a
 13        WHERE  col_1 LIKE '%,%'
 14        OR     col_1 LIKE '%-%')
 15    LOOP
 16      v_val := r.val;
 17      FOR i IN 1 .. r.num LOOP
 18        IF SUBSTR (v_val, 1, INSTR (v_val, ',') - 1) NOT
LIKE '%-%' THEN
 19          INSERT INTO tbl_a (col_1)
 20          VALUES (LTRIM (RTRIM (SUBSTR (v_val, 1,
INSTR (v_val, ',') - 1))));
 21        ELSE
 22          v_first := LTRIM (RTRIM (SUBSTR (v_val, 1,
INSTR (v_val, '-') - 1)));
 23          v_last := SUBSTR (v_val, INSTR (v_val, '-') +
1);
 24          v_last := LTRIM (RTRIM (SUBSTR (v_last, 1,
INSTR (v_last, ',') - 1)));
```

```
25      FOR j IN TO_NUMBER (v_first) .. TO_NUMBER
(v_last) LOOP
26          INSERT INTO tbl_a (col_1) VALUES (j);
27        END LOOP;
28      END IF;
29      v_val := SUBSTR (v_val, INSTR (v_val, ',') + 1);
30      END LOOP;
31    END LOOP;
32
33    DELETE FROM tbl_a
34    WHERE   col_1 LIKE '%,%'
35    OR    col_1 LIKE '%-%';
36  END remove_groups;
37  /
```

Procedure created.

scott@ORA92> SHOW ERRORS
No errors.
scott@ORA92> EXECUTE remove_groups

PL/SQL procedure successfully completed.

scott@ORA92> SELECT col_1 FROM tbl_a
  2 /

COL_1

225
221
222
41
42
43
44

45
49
332
333
334
335
336
337
211
63
64
65
66

20 rows selected.

This procedure can lessen your work hours from months into minutes.

☞ QUESTION 57

Looping through lines

I am trying to match cpt codes in table A to find a matching pair in table B. Any of the cpt codes in table A may match the codes in table B, but they must match as a pair in table B.

Table A
Claimno 888888
Claimline 01
Cpt code 123456
Claimline 02
Cpt code 123457
Claimline 03
Cpt code 897689

Table B
Primary CPT Secondary CPT
123456 123457
5766849 123457

So line 1 in table B would be the matching code pair because there are two cpt codes in table A that match the pair in line one of table B. I am not sure how to loop through the claim lines to find the pair, or if a simple join would do the trick.

✎ ANSWER

Your requirement can be achieved by:

SELECT * FROM TAB_B B
WHERE EXISTS (SELECT NULL
        FROM   TAB_A A

```
        WHERE  B.primary_cpt = A.cpt_code)
AND EXISTS  (SELECT NULL
        FROM TAB_A C
        WHERE B.sec_cpt=C.cpt_code);
```

OR

```
SELECT B.*
 FROM   TAB_A A ,TAB_B B ,TAB_A C
 WHERE  B.primary_cpt = A.cpt_code(+)
 AND    B.sec_cpt    = C.cpt_code(+)
 AND    A.cpt_code IS NOT NULL
 AND    C.cpt_code IS NOT NULL;
```

OR SIMPLY BY,

```
 SELECT B.* FROM  TAB_B B, TAB_A A ,TAB_A C
 WHERE B.primary_cpt=A.cpt_code
 AND   B.sec_cpt = C.cpt_code;
```

☞ QUESTION **58**

Remove a Specific Character

I want to remove a specific character from a column.

For example:

Tbl_A
Col_1
xx123
787xxx
77xxx554

I want to remove all leading, trailing and middle 'x' from Col_1.

How can I do it effectively?

✍ ANSWER

UPDATE tbl_a;
SET   col_1 = REPLACE(col_1,'x');

☞ QUESTION 59

No need for cursors

I have actually achieved the functionality, but I want to verify it.

My requirement was to have a table like this:

Name Type
NAME VARCHAR2(10)
VAL1 NUMBER(9,2)
VAL2 NUMBER(9,2)
MYDATE DATE

I have another table with more or less the same structure. I have to calculate average of val1 and val2 columns and insert all data into table2.

The procedure I used was:

"create or replace procedure ins_inmacs is
begin insert into tbl_inmacs1 select name, val1,val2,(val1+val2)/2 from tbl_inmacs;
commit;
end;"

This is a simple procedure but it is satisfying my requirement.

My question is if there is any need for a cursor here?

✍ ANSWER

You are correct; there is no need for a cursor here. As a matter of fact, this means of INSERT that you've described would be the preferred method.

☞ QUESTION **60**

Exception which violates primary key constraint

My table has a primary key combination of 3 columns.

I want to insert into the table, if the row with same primary key combination does not exist in the table. If the row with the same primary key combination already exists in the table, then I want to update that row.

Can you please let me know the exception that would arise when inserting a row that violates primary key constraint?

✍ ANSWER

Here is the exception:

"ORA-00001: Unique constraint (schema_name.contrant_name) violated";

It seems you are going to write a pl/sql for the above, but there is already a facility offered by Oracle, faster and simpler. It is called the "Merge command".

Look here for an applicable MERGE Statement:
http://www.oracle.com/technology/products/oracle9i/daily/apr30.html;

Quote:

"Prior to Oracle9i, these operations were expressed either as a sequence of DMLs (INSERT/UPDATE) or as PL/SQL loops deciding, for each row, whether to insert or update the data. Both these techniques face performance handicaps: the first requires multiple data scans, and the second operates on a per-record basis. By extending SQL with a new syntax - the MERGE statement - Oracle9i overcomes the deficiencies of the old approaches and makes the implementation of warehousing applications more simple and intuitive".

☞ QUESTION 61

Package dependency - recompile

I've got the following situation in a productive environment here:

- A package A with a procedure P1
- A package B with a procedure P2

Please note that the interface is altered too.

Is it possible to recompile package A without making package B invalid?

✍ ANSWER

Does 'ALTER PACKAGE B COMPILE BODY' work for you? This leaves the specification as it is, so the dependency chain is broken.

It shouldn't be too much of a problem, if the calls from B to A are still valid. B gets recompiled automatically when it is called the first time.

☞ QUESTION 62

Input variable character

I input into my stored procedure: runtestcode IN
VARCHAR;

runtestcode max input values are '1,2,3,4,5,6,7'
testcodes 6 and 7 are the same tests, so when I get 6 and 7 as
input i need to run one test only.

Meaning if I get input as '1,2,3,4,5,6,7', my where clause
should contain '1,2,3,4,5,6' removing 7;

Similarly if I get '6, 7' as input I should use 6 only. Is there any
function which I can use to solve it?

✍ ANSWER

If you are passing string as an input or individual values, and
if you're input in 1 or 2 or 3 or 4 or 5 or 6 or 7, then you can
create or replace procedure as:

runtest(runtestcode varchar2)

Begin if runtestcode in ('1','2','3','4','5') then

runtest;(u r code to run the)

else

if runtestcode in ('6','7') then

```
runtest6;
end if;

exception handling;

end;
```

An alternative would be to use a combination of CASE, INSTR and SUBSTR:

```
var thestring varchar2(20)

exec :thestring := '1,2,3,4,5,6 , 7,8'
col thestring format A20
col thetest format A20

SELECT thestring
   , CASE
     WHEN INSTR (thestring,'6') > 0
     THEN
      CASE
      WHEN INSTR (thestring,'7,') > 0
      THEN
        SUBSTR ( thestring, 1, INSTR(thestring,'7,')-1)
       ||SUBSTR (thestring,INSTR(thestring,'7,')+2)
      WHEN INSTR (thestring,'7') > 0
      THEN
        SUBSTR ( thestring, 1, INSTR(thestring,'7')-2)
      ELSE
       thestring
      END
     ELSE
      thestring
      END thetest
   FROM (SELECT -- remove blanks
```

```
    REPLACE (TRANSLATE (:thestring,' ',CHR(1)),CHR(1),'')
thestring
      FROM dual
   )
/

exec :thestring := '1,2,3,4,5,6  , 7'

/
```

This results in the following output:

SQL> @C:\useful\orafaq

PL/SQL procedure successfully completed.

```
THESTRING          THETEST
------------------ ------------------
1,2,3,4,5,6,7,8    1,2,3,4,5,6,8
```

PL/SQL procedure successfully completed.

```
THESTRING          THETEST
------------------ ------------------
1,2,3,4,5,6,7      1,2,3,4,5,6
```

SQL>

It has limitations; it removes every occurrence of '7' if a single '6' is present. '17' becomes '1' but it can get you started.

☞ QUESTION 63

Trigger creating two rows rather than just one

I am struggling to understand why my trigger is creating two records when I am updating only one column.

Objects Description:

1) TEMP table has got two columns OLD_SCAN, NEW_SCAN
2) IF OLD_SCAN, NEW_SCAN column is changed then it should insert record in TEMP_TEST table.

Expectation:
1. I have created oracle forms which insert/update records in TEMP_TEST table.
2. When I update "OLD_SCAN" column via form then it should only fire ONE trigger, and should only insert "hello" value in "temp_test"
3. In the same way if I update new_scan column then it should only fire "TWO" trigger and insert "HI" in TEMP_TEST table.

4. Currently it is inserting two records; HI and Hello into temp_test table, regardless if you update NEW_SCAN column or OLD_SCAN column.

Please suggest what I am doing wrong
Here is code below:

CREATE OR REPLACE TRIGGER one

AFTER
INSERT OR UPDATE OF old_scan
ON temp
REFERENCING NEW AS NEW OLD AS OLD
FOR EACH ROW
Begin
if updating('OLD_SCAN') THEN
insert into temp_test values ('Hello');
END IF;
END;

CREATE OR REPLACE TRIGGER two AFTER
INSERT OR UPDATE OF new_scan
ON temp
REFERENCING NEW AS NEW OLD AS OLD
FOR EACH ROW
Begin
if updating('New_scan') THEN
insert into temp_test values ('HI');
END if;
END;

How do I resolve this?

✍ Answer

The update trigger also fires if you update a column to its old value. This is probably what Forms does, it updates the entire row, setting old_scan to x and new_scan to y.

If you only alter old_scan, it still updates new_scan to y (being the original value).

SQL> create table t (a number, b number);

Table created.

SQL> create or replace trigger t_trg
  2 before insert or update on t
  3 for each row
  4 begin
  5   if updating ('b') then
  6   dbms_output.put_line('Updating b');
  7   else
  8   dbms_output.put_line('Not updating b');
  9   end if;
 10 end;
 11 /

Trigger created.

SQL> insert into t values (1, 2);
Not updating b

1 row created.

SQL> update t set b = 3;
Updating b

1 row updated.

SQL> /
Updating b

1 row updated. Report message to a moderator.

You might also want to check whether you have set the "update changed columns only" property on the block.

☞ QUESTION 64

Can't call PL/SQL Package in VB

We have a PL/SQL reference cursor that returns values from the Oracle table. We need to pass these values to MS Access tables using VB Code.

We created ODBC connection and were able to retrieve records from Oracle table in MS ACCESS. Now we need to retrieve cursor values. For that we are using the following code:

Option Explicit:

Public m_adoCnn As New ADODB.Connection

Public Sub Command0_Click()
Dim sSQL As String
Dim m_adoRst As ADODB.Recordset
Dim m_adoCmd As ADODB.Command
Dim m_adoPrm As ADODB.Parameter

sSQL = "emp_hist_refcur.empsearch"
Set m_adoCmd = New ADODB.Command
With m_adoCnn
'.ConnectionString = "DSN=TGFSDBA_Test;Pwd=tgfsdba_ot35;UID=tgfsdba"
.ConnectionString = "Provider=msdaora;Data Source=TGFSDBA_Test;" & _
"User ID=tgfsdba;Password=tgfsdba_ot35;PLSQLRSet=1;"

.CursorLocation = adUseServer

.Open
End With

With m_adoCmd
.ActiveConnection = m_adoCnn
.CommandType = adCmdStoredProc
.CommandText = sSQL
'.Parameters.Refresh
' Set m_adoPrm = .CreateParameter("pTest", advarChar, adParamInput, 1)
'.Parameters.Append m_adoPrm
End With
'm_adoPrm.Value = "x"
Set m_adoRst = m_adoCmd.Execute

End Sub

Private Sub Form_Unload(Cancel As Integer)
m_adoCnn.Close
End Sub

When we run it, it gives us a "TNSNAMES.ORA could not be resolved" error, and it highlights ".OPEN" in the code?

What could be wrong?

When we run it using this connection string
'.ConnectionString = "DSN=TGFSDBA_Test;Pwd=tgfsdba_ot35;UID=tgfsdba"

Then we get an error saying: "Wrong number or type of arguments in a call"

Do we need to configure TNSNAMES, install a driver, or try a new connection string like OO4O instead of ADO?

✍ Answer

Find the entire tnsnames.ora file on your machine (ignore the ones under ...\sample\). You can rename copies of tnsnames. ora to something else, so you can identify which one VB is trying to access. You should be able to set environment variable TNS_ADMIN to point to the path of the master copy of tnsnames.ora, you want all Oracle calls to use.

http://asktom.oracle.com/~tkyte/ResultSets/

☞ QUESTION **65**

Single Column Multiple Row Data

Suppose I have a comma separated string and I want to put them in a single column multiple row array.

I am passed a string say:
ls_variable = '23754,23638,23729,23630'

I want to show it as:

23754
23638
23729
23630

I want basically to put it in one column with multiple rows. I want it to be SQL.

How can I write a sql for that?

✍ ANSWER

Here is one way to do it:

```
SQL> VARIABLE to_split VARCHAR2(30)
SQL> VARIABLE delim    VARCHAR2(1)
SQL> EXEC :to_split := '23754,23638,23729,23630'; :delim :=
',';
```

PL/SQL procedure successfully completed.

```
SQL> SELECT    a.n
 2  ,        SUBSTR(:to_split
 3           ,    INSTR(:delim
 4                    || :to_split
 5                    || :delim
 6               ,    :delim
 7               ,    1
 8               ,    a.n)
 9           ,    INSTR(:delim
10                    || :to_split
11                    || :delim
12               ,    :delim
13               ,    1
14               ,    a.n + 1)
15                -
16                INSTR(:delim
17                    || :to_split
18                    || :delim
19               ,    :delim
20               ,    1
21               ,    a.n) - 1)  piece
22  FROM    (SELECT    LEVEL    n
23          FROM    DUAL
24          CONNECT BY LEVEL <= LENGTH(:to_split)
25                -
26                    LENGTH(REPLACE(:to_split,:delim))
+ 1) a
27  /
```

```
      N PIECE
--------- ---------------------------
      1 23754
      2 23638
      3 23729
      4 23630
```

SQL>And another:
SQL> VARIABLE to_split VARCHAR2(30)
SQL> EXEC :to_split := '23754,23638,23729,23630';

PL/SQL procedure successfully completed.

SQL> CREATE OR REPLACE TYPE tt_v2 AS TABLE OF VARCHAR2(255)
  2 /

Type created.

```
SQL> CREATE OR REPLACE FUNCTION string_to_table (
  2    p_str    IN  VARCHAR2
  3 , p_delim    IN  VARCHAR2 DEFAULT ','
  4 )
  5 RETURN tt_v2
  6 PIPELINED
  7 AS
  8    l_str   VARCHAR2(32700) DEFAULT p_str || p_delim;
  9    l_n    PLS_INTEGER;
 10 BEGIN
 11    LOOP
 12      l_n := INSTR(l_str, p_delim);
 13      EXIT WHEN (NVL(l_n,0) = 0);
 14      PIPE ROW (TRIM(SUBSTR(l_str,1,l_n - 1)));
 15      l_str := SUBSTR(l_str, l_n + 1);
 16    END LOOP;
 17    RETURN;
 18 END string_to_table;
 19 /
```

Function created.

SQL> SELECT column_value

```
2 FROM  TABLE(string_to_table(:to_split))
3 /
```

COLUMN_VALUE

23754
23638
23729
23630

SQL>

☞ QUESTION **66**

Pass a ref cursor value from Oracle to MS access Database

We have created a stored procedure with a ref cursor that returns values from an Oracle table. We have been able to do it successfully.

Now we want to dump these values returned by the ref cursor in Oracle to a table in MS Access.

I have never worked with MS Access Database before.

I have 2 questions:

How would we connect MS Access to Oracle?

How would we go about retrieving records from ref cursor in PL/SQL stored procedure and populating it in the table that we created in MS Access?

✍ ANSWER

This is surely an access question. Use ODBC to connect to oracle, and make a call to the procedure.

You could further check out www.utteraccess.com to see if you can get more options there.

☞ QUESTION 67

Execution of scripts

I wanted to execute 5 scripts, namely a.sql, b.sql, c.sql, d.sql, e.sql.

1> I wanted to execute these 5 scripts in single shot.

Is there a preferred method with which I can do this?

2> If any of the scripts fail, how do I trace which scripts have failed?

✍ ANSWER

Create a runall.sql

@/user/abc/a.sql
@/user/abc/b.sql
@/user/abc/c.sql
@/user/abc/d.sql
@/user/abc/e.sql

I am not sure how to trap the error here. Use a spool and see which statements fail. Or you could write to a file (or screen).

An alternative approach is to have a look at the WHENEVER SQLERROR or WHENEVER OSERROR clause of SQL*Plus. You can include it in your scripts and perform specified actions if sql or operating system error occurs.

http://download-west.oracle.com/docs/cd/B10501_01/
server.920/a90842/ch13.htm#1014742

☞ QUESTION 68

Erroneous trigger

I have created a trigger in oracle 8.1, running it at 10g trigger is:

create or replace trigger trig_event after insert on tbl_field_valchange
declare cursor incrs is SELECT   field_newvalue from tbl_field_valchange where field_newvalue like '%~%' and (LENGTH(field_newvalue)-NVL(LENGTH(REPLACE(field_newvalue,'~',''))),0))/LENGTH('~') =4;
  v_vals tbl_field_valchange.field_newvalue%type;
  v_errorcode number;
  v_errortext varchar2(300);
begin

  open incrs;
  loop
fetch incrs into v_vals;
exit when incrs%notfound;
    insert into tbl_modemevents(fault_type,fault_code,fault_indicator,fault_date,fault_time)
  values(substr(v_vals,1,instr(v_vals,'~')-1),
        substr(v_vals,instr(v_vals,'~')+1,instr(v_vals,'~',1,2)-1-instr(v_vals,'~')),
          substr(v_vals,instr(v_vals,'~',1,2)+1,instr(v_vals,'~',1,3)-1-instr(v_vals,'~',1,2)),
          substr(v_vals,instr(v_vals,'~',1,3)+1,instr(v_vals,'~',1,4)-1-instr(v_vals,'~',1,3)),
          substr(v_vals,instr(v_vals,'~',1,4)+1,instr(v_vals,'~',1,5)-1-instr(v_vals,'~',1,4)));

```
  end loop;
  close incrs;
  exception
  when no_data_found then
  dbms_output.put_line('there is no data');
  when others then
  v_errorcode:=sqlcode;
  v_errortext:=sqlerrm;
  dbms_output.put_line('Error code is 'llv_errorcodell' and
  message is ' llv_errortext);
  end;
```

ddl is

```
create table tbl_field_valchange (field_id number(10) not
null, field_devicename varchar2(100) not null, field_name
varchar2(100)   not   null,   field_oldvalue   varchar2(100),
field_newvalue   varchar2(100),   field_date   date,   incbkp
number(3))
```

```
create table tbl_modemevents (field_id number(10) not null,
EVENT_DEVICENAME varchar2(100) not null, CURRENT_
DATE   date,   FAULT_TYPE   varchar2(40),   FAULT_CODE
varchar2(40),   FAULT_INDICATOR   varchar2(40),   FAULT_
DATE   varchar2(40),   FAULT_TIME   varchar2(40),   incbkp
number(3))
```

tbl_field_valchange is the source table, in that table,
the   field   field_newvalue   has   data   like
'abc~xyz~yuy~nmn~nnn'
it has 4 tilts (~)
the   trigger   should   extract   abc,   and   insert   into   tbl_
modemevents
fault_type column, insert xyz into tbl_modemevents fault_
code column and so on

The trigger is created, but data is not inserted into target table.

Why is it happening?

How can this be resolved?

✍ ANSWER

The following is your insert statements:

Quote:

Insert into tbl_modemevents(fault_type,fault_code,fault_indicator,fault_date,fault_time)

But, your DDL statements have indicated that you must have field_id number and EVENT_DEVICENAME!

Quote:

create table tbl_modemevents (field_id number(10) not null, EVENT_DEVICENAME varchar2(100) not null, ...

So to correct it, insert these 2 values:

INSERTINTOtbl_modemevents(field_id, event_devicename, fault_type, fault_code, fault_indicator, fault_date, fault_time)
...

☞ QUESTION 69

BLOB

I have a table which is having BLOB data type columns. My requirement is to retrieve the values from that column and store it as file (pdf).

If I use the below statement it is giving output as 1173.

SELECT DBMS_LOB.getlength(blob_file) FROM STORE_BLOB

How can I retrieve the values?

✐ ANSWER

Look in the PL/SQL reference manual.

Good examples or BLOB/CLOB use dbms_lob package.

This can be found in stored procedure/package.

☞ QUESTION 70

Use the package DBMS_TRANSACTION

I do a lot of PL/SQL in my job but I have not used this package.

If there is any advantage to be gained by using this package, I would like to try it.

Can you provide me a list of situations that would warrant use of this package?

✍ ANSWER

It depends on the Version of Oracle. Version 8i is used to specify rollback segment. The dbms_transaction.set_rollback_segment was used for large ETL load.

With 9i UNDO space makes this less valuable.

.read_only if you want to ensure a read only session.

.commit .rollback .rollback_savepoint .savpoint are obvious and be handled with SQL syntax

commit_comment - if you need a comment for trace?

The built-in package document should have the complete use details.

☞ QUESTION 71

Numeric or value error

I have written shell script with pl/sql script in it-here is pl/sql part:

```
POM="set serveroutput on;
DECLARE
foutput VARCHAR(4);
status VARCHAR(4);
id NUMBER;
billday NUMBER;

BEGIN

-- Now call the stored program
foutput := eb_api.f_User_Get("421905111111",id,billday,stat
us);
-- Output the results
dbms_output.put_line(SubStr('id    =    '||TO_CHAR(id),   1,
255));
dbms_output.put_line(SubStr('billday        =        '||TO_
CHAR(billday), 1, 255));
dbms_output.put_line('status = '||status);
dbms_output.put_line(SubStr('foutput = '||foutput, 1, 255));
COMMIT;

EXCEPTION
WHEN OTHERS THEN
dbms_output.put_line(SubStr('Error              '||TO_
CHAR(SQLCODE)||': '||SQLERRM, 1, 255));

RAISE;
```

END;

/
"

Script returns this output:
SQL*Plus: Release 8.1.7.0.0 - Production on Fri Jan 20 14:58:36 2006

(c) Copyright 2000 Oracle Corporation. All rights reserved.

Connected to:
Oracle8i Enterprise Edition Release 8.1.7.0.0 - Production
With the Partitioning option
JServer Release 8.1.7.0.0 - Production

SQL> SQL> 2 3 4 5 6 7 8 9 10 11 12 13 14 15
16 17 18 19 20 21 22 23 24 25 Error -6502: ORA-06502: PL/SQL
: numeric or value error: character to number
conversion error
DECLARE
*
ERROR at line 1:
ORA-06502: PL/SQL: numeric or value error: character to number conversion error
ORA-06512: at line 22

SQL> SQL> Disconnected from Oracle8i Enterprise Edition Release 8.1.7.0.0 - Production
With the Partitioning option
JServer Release 8.1.7.0.0 - Production

I tried to declare variables in many combinations, but I can't get through this error.

How do I proceed from here?

✍ ANSWER

You can temporarily remove the exception handler to see the REAL line number where the error occurs.

Line 22 now points to the RAISE.

Something like this:

```
dbms_output.put_line(SubStr('Error                    'IITO_
CHAR(SQLCODE)II ': 'IISQLERRM), 1, 255);
?
```

SubStr function has 3 arguments so i think it should be correct. I've tried it and this is the output:
PLS-00306: wrong number or types of arguments in call to 'SUBSTR';

☞ QUESTION 72

Overcoming Mutating Table Error

What is the solution for overcoming Mutating Table Error?

✍ ANSWER

You are encountering the infamous 'mutating table' problem.

The source of the problem is that you are trying to read from a table while you are changing it. Oracle can no longer guarantee read consistency and therefore it raises the ORA 4091.

Here's an excerpt of a document I once created:

"Oracle Mutating Table Problem and how to avoid it

What is the Mutating Table Problem exactly?

A mutating table is a table that is currently being modified by an update, delete, or insert statement. You will encounter the ORA-4091 error if you have a row trigger that reads or modifies the mutating table.

A constraining table is a table that a triggering statement might need to read either directly, for a SQL statement, or indirectly, for a declarative referential integrity constraint. A table is mutating or constraining only to the session that issued the statement in progress.

For example, if your trigger contains a select statement or an update statement referencing the table it is triggering off of you will receive the error. Another way this error can occur is if the trigger has statements to change the primary, foreign or unique key columns of the table the trigger is triggering off of.

If you must have triggers on tables that have referential constraints, the workaround is to enforce the referential integrity through triggers as well.

Assume that you have table EMP(empno, ename, sal, deptno):

EMPNO	ENAME	SAL	DEPTNO
00001	BECKER	1000	10
00002	JONES	1250	10
...			
00503	WARNER	1025	95

This table has an AFTER ROW INSERT/UPDATE trigger that verifies that a certain maximum of the total salaries is not yet met:
...
...
Begin
  Select sum(sal)
    Into v_total
    From emp;
...
....

Now, imagine that you perform the following update:
UPDATE EMP SET SAL = SAL*1.1;

Notice that the SQL statement is run for the first row of

the table, and then an AFTER row trigger is fired. In turn, a statement in the AFTER row trigger body attempts to query the original table. However, because the EMP table is mutating (the content has already changed) , this query is not allowed by Oracle. If attempted, then a runtime error occurs, the effects of the trigger body and triggering statement are rolled back, and control is returned to the user or application.

How can I avoid a mutating table?

If you need to update a mutating or constraining table, then you could use a temporary table, a PL/SQL table, or a package variable to bypass these restrictions.

For example, in place of a single AFTER row trigger that updates the original table, resulting in a mutating table error, you may be able to use two triggers. The first is an AFTER row trigger that updates a temporary table, and the second an AFTER statement trigger that updates the original table with the values from the temporary table.

For example:

Consider table:

EMPLOYEES (employee_id number, department_id number, name varchar2 (20), wage number);

If one creates a before insert or update trigger which checks that the total of wages for a department doesnï¿œt exceed 2 million Belgian Francs.

One could say:

```
CREATE TRIGGER BRUI_EMPLOYEES

BEFORE INSERT OR UPDATE ON Employees

FOR EACH ROW

DECLARE

        CURSOR c_wages

        IS SELECT count(wages) total_wages

        WHERE department_id = :NEW.department_id

        FROM EMPLOYEES;

        v_total_wages NUMBER;

BEGIN

        OPEN c_wages;

        FETCH c_wages INTO v_total_wages;

        CLOSE c_wages;

        IF v_total_wages > 2000000 THEN
-- do exception handling
```

-- Some exception package is being called

PCK$EXCEPTIONS.RAISE('Total   wages   exceeds budget');
END IF;
END;

We issue the following command after creating the trigger:

SQL>UPDATE employees

   SET wage = 14500

   WHERE id = 6;

This command will fail. It will result in an ORA-4091 error, since we were trying to read the table while we modify it.

Therefore, we need to adjust the processing a little bit:

Create a package specification. The body is not necessary at this time, since we don't do any actual processing in the package itself, and it doesn't need to contain any logic.
CREATE OR REPLACE PACKAGE pck$mutations

IS

      Gv_department_id NUMBER; -- global variable

END pck$mutations; Create a before insert/update trigger for each row to store the department id in the global variable.
CREATE TRIGGER BRUI_EMPLOYEES

BEFORE INSERT OR UPDATE ON Employees

FOR EACH ROW

BEGIN

   Pck$mutations.Gv_department_id   :=:NEW.
department_id; -- store

--department id in global variable

   END;Create an after insert/update statement trigger do
the actual check.
CREATE TRIGGER ASUI_EMPLOYEES

AFTER INSERT OR UPDATE ON Employees

DECLARE

      CURSOR c_wages

      IS SELECT count(wages) total_wages

         WHERE   department_id   =   pck$mutations.
department_id

      FROM EMPLOYEES;

      v_total_wages NUMBER;

```
BEGIN

     OPEN c_wages;

     FETCH c_wages INTO v_total_wages;

     CLOSE c_wages;

     IF v_total_wages > 2000000 THEN
-- do exception handling

-- some exception package is being called

     PCK$EXCEPTIONS.RAISE('Total   wages   exceeds
budget');
  END IF;
END;
```

To summarize: If one encounters a mutating table issue, he/she should do basically the following:

Create a package header to contain any: NEW or: OLD values that are necessary to perform checks.

Create a before each row trigger that fills these variables.

Create an after statement trigger that performs the checks.

Useful remarks:

An after statement trigger fires before any changes are saved to the database. If the trigger fails/raises an error, all changes of that transaction are rolled back.

When processing so-called bulk inserts/updates, the system might need PL/SQL tables to contain the variables. This is due to the fact that a row level trigger fires for each row, (i.e. possibly more times in a bulk operation) and a statement trigger fires only once per statement (hence the names). In the before row trigger one should insert a record in the PL/SQL table. In the after statement trigger, loop through the records of the PL/SQL table and do the necessary processing.

Useful internet addresses: Oracle Technology Network (OTN), the technical website of Oracle corporation. http://otn.oracle.com or http://technet.oracle.com Oracle support: Metalink (requires support Id and password): http://metalink.oracle.com

You could add the package body PCK$MUT, to write a sort of API around the variable and make it hidden for calling triggers. That way, no one can directly access the variable. You could write a SET_VAR procedure to fill the variable, a GET_VAR function to retrieve the value of the variable, a CLEAR_VAR procedure to empty the variable."

End of quote.

If this is not clear you can always search for 'Mutating table' or http://asktom.oracle.com (Tom Kytes' website, a site to put in your favorites). I strongly recommend looking at AskTom. Usually he's very clear and uses straightforward examples.

☞ QUESTION **73**

Procedures for calling function

I created this function to handle the calling of procedures in packages and it works just fine for procedures, but it doesn't seem to work for calling functions (IsGenerator) in a package, so I want to create another function called ExecFunction. I'm not quite sure what I have to change.

Do I change the command type, or do I change the SQL passed in?

I've tried a sql of "begin: RETURN: = EQUIPMENT. IsGenerator(:n_CCA_NUM); end;" with a command type of text and that didn't work. It didn't produce an error, but the return value was 0 instead of the hard coded value of 100 in the function.

PrivateConst_PackageNameAddAsString="GENERATORS. ADD_REC"

This is the calling function that developers coded:

Private Sub Add (ByVal R As GeneratorsDataset.C_ GENERATORSRow)
Dim Ps as New Utilities.DBManager.Parameters
Ps.Add("n_cca_num", R.CCA_NUM, Int32, Input)
Ps.Add("v_ccs", R.CCS, Varchar2, Input)
Dim OutputPs as New Utilities.DBManager.Parameters
OutputPs = _DB.ExecProcedure(_PackageNameAdd, Ps)
End Sub

Utility function:

```
Public Function ExecProcedure(ByVal SQL As String, ByVal
Parms As DBManager.Parameters) As Parameters
If _Conn.State = ConnectionState.Closed Or _Conn.State =
ConnectionState.Broken Then _Conn.Open()
Dim    cmd    As    New    Oracle.DataAccess.Client.
OracleCommand(SQL, _Conn)
cmd.CommandType = CommandType.StoredProcedure
Dim P As DBManager.Parameters.Parameter
'add parms to ADO parm collection
If Not (Parms Is Nothing) Then
For Each P in Parms
Debug.Write(P.Name & " = " & P.Value & ", ")
cmd.Parameters.Add(P.Name, P.type, P.Value, P.Direction)
Next
End If
'Run package
cmd.ExecuteNonQuery()
Dim OutputDataTables as New Parameters
'loop through all parms and find all output and add to
collection
If Not (Parms Is Nothing) Then
For Each P In Parms
If P.Direction = ParameterDirection.Output Or P.Direction =
ParameterDirection.ReturnValue Then
P.Value = cmd.Parameters(P.Name)
OutputDataTables.Add(P)
End If
Next
End If
_Conn.Close()
'return collection of output
Return OutputDataTables
End Function
```

How do I correct the error?

✍ ANSWER

If you do the following changes and re-configuration:

Caller

```
Private Sub Button1_Click(ByVal sender As System.Object,
ByVal e As System.EventArgs) Handles Button1.Click
Dim ps as New Parameters
Dim Outs as New Parameters
Try
ps.Add("n_CCA_NUM",    5,    Oracle.DataAccess.Client.
OracleDbType.Int32, ParameterDirection.Input)
Me.TextBox2.Text = CType(ExecFunction(Me.TextBox1.
Text, ps), String)
Catch ee As Exception
MsgBox(ee.ToString)
End Try
End Sub
```

Utility

```
Public Function ExecFunction(ByVal PackageName As
String, ByVal Parms As Parameters) As Object
If _Conn.State = ConnectionState.Closed Or _Conn.State =
ConnectionState.Broken Then _Conn.Open()
PackageName = "SELECT" & PackageName & "("

Dim P As Parameters.Parameter
'add parms to ADO parm collection
If Not (Parms Is Nothing) Then
For Each P In Parms
PackageName = PackageName & ":" & P.Name & ","
```

```
Next
End If
PackageName = PackageName.Substring(0, PackageName.
Length - 2) & ") FROM DUAL"

Dim cmd As New Oracle.DataAccess.Client.OracleComman
d(PackageName, _Conn)
cmd.CommandType = CommandType.Text
'add parms to ADO parm collection
If Not (Parms Is Nothing) Then
For Each P In Parms
cmd.Parameters.Add(P.Name, P.type, P.Value, P.Direction)
Next
End If
'run package
ExecFunction = cmd.ExecuteScalar
_Conn.Close()
End Function
```

This one fails if there is an output parameter.

Below is the proper way to call a function that is inside an oracle package from VB.net using Oracle's provider:

This is the new utility function that works.

```
Public          Function          ExecPackageFunction(ByVal
PackageAndFunctionName  As  String,  ByVal  Parms  As
Parameters) As Parameters
     '  Author:        Franklin Gray
     '  Created Date:  9/29/2005
     '  Purpose:       Call an Oracle package function and
return the return value
     '
     '  Process:       Create parm collection
     '                 Call package
```

'   Load output parms into collection
'

'   Input: package name and collection of
parameters
'   Output: return value
'

'   Changes: (who, what, where, and when)
'

If _Conn.State = ConnectionState.Closed Or _Conn.State
= ConnectionState.Broken Then _Conn.Open()
    PackageAndFunctionName = "declare RET INT; BEGIN
:RET := " & PackageAndFunctionName & "("

    Dim P As DBManager.Parameters.Parameter, Outputs As
New DBManager.Parameters
    'add parms to ADO parm collection
    If Not (Parms Is Nothing) Then
        For Each P In Parms
IfNotP.Direction=ParameterDirection.ReturnValueThen
PackageAndFunctionName = PackageAndFunctionName &
":" & P.Name & ","
        Next
    End If

    PackageAndFunctionName = PackageAndFunctionName.
Substring(0, PackageAndFunctionName.Length - 2) & ");
END;"

    Dim cmd As New Oracle.DataAccess.Client.OracleCom
mand(PackageAndFunctionName, _Conn)
    cmd.CommandType = CommandType.Text
    'add parms to ADO parm collection

    If Not (Parms Is Nothing) Then
        For Each P In Parms
            'Debug.Write(P.Name & " = " & P.Value & ", ")

```
Dim L As Int32
If P.Size > 0 Then
    L = P.Size
Else
    If P.Value Is System.DBNull.Value Then
        L = 1
    Else
        L = Len(P.Value)
    End If
End If
    cmd.Parameters.Add(P.Name, P.type, L, P.Value,
P.Direction)
        If P.Direction = ParameterDirection.Output Or
P.Direction = ParameterDirection.ReturnValue Then Outputs.
Add(P)
    Next
End If
'run package
cmd.ExecuteScalar()
Dim OutputDataTables As New Parameters
'loop through all parms and find all output and add to
collection
If Not (Outputs Is Nothing) Then
    For Each P In Outputs
        If P.Direction = ParameterDirection.Output Or
P.Direction = ParameterDirection.ReturnValue Then
            P.Value = cmd.Parameters(P.Name).Value
            OutputDataTables.Add(P)
        End If
    Next
End If
ExecPackageFunction = OutputDataTables
cmd.Dispose()
End Function
```

☞ QUESTION 74

PL/SQL initialize ()

I am looking into creating a JAVA-like delegator layer in PL/SQL. For example, the top-layer will call other packages that performs the actual business logic i.e. search, update.

For example:
1. Check if all low-level packages are compiled and in a good state;
2. Check for errors;
3. Other

My objective is to have the delegator package contain a LONG list of APIs to other packages. I also would like to make sure that the delegator package is easy to maintain and debug if something goes wrong with the other dependent packages.

What "things" should I consider while initializing the top-level package?

✍ ANSWER

The connection is thru the schema owner of packages. It would need select count (*) from all_objects where owner='your objects owner' where status <> 'VALID'

If you can re-validate if count>0. By reference it will recompile but persistent connection may say it's still invalid.

Use   dbms_utility.compile_schema('your   object owner',false);

Which compiles invalid only object. This assumes your connection is allowed to do this.

You may have to run it more than once if cross referenced objects are invalid.

The things that you have to consider in initializing is dependent on delagator's package "other" requirements. It may have other application specific requirements.

For example:

Table values to control version of client and auto upgrade end user as needed.

Do you trigger control of how and where users login from v$session checks?

At this how much configuration and control/health checking do you want?

One big consideration for all of these requirements will be the security budget that is actually allocated.

If the budget is limited, you can always add functionality as you go along.

For the meantime, please take note that the PL/SQL is invoked by a new request from the JAVA application server.

Here is an example: UI user performs "info search" operation > JAVA method () > PL/SQL Top.searchInfo() > PL/SQL

Search.do().

Somewhere in the PL/SQL body of Top:
-- Schema version check is done
-- Compilation is done
-- Validation check is done
-- If problems with Validation, report errors back to JAVA App log
-- Enable Profiling and Tracing PL/SQL from JAVA

☞ QUESTION **75**

PLS-00049 - Bad bind variable

While compiling the following trigger I always get the PLS-00049 mistake (Bad bind variable). I also check all listed columns on data type and spelling.

PLSQL-Developer always jumps to the first listed: New-Parameter in my Trigger-Text.

For example:

```
CREATE OR REPLACE TRIGGER TBFBDI_OFFENE_
POSTEN_AFT_INS
AFTER INSERT ON TBFBDI_OFFENE_POSTEN
FOR EACH ROW
DECLARE
vBELEGART          VARCHAR2(4);
vSTEUERSCHLUESSEL    VARCHAR2(2);
vGEGENKONTONUMMER    VARCHAR2(12);
vBUCHUNGSBETRAG      VARCHAR2(16);
BEGIN
        IF :NEW.KONTONUMMER >= 10000 AND :NEW.
KONTONUMMER < 70000 THEN
    vBELEGART := 'OPID';
    vGEGENKONTONUMMER := '9008';
        ELSIF :NEW.KONTONUMMER >= 70000 AND :NEW.
KONTONUMMER < 100000 THEN
    vBELEGART := 'OPIK';
    vGEGENKONTONUMMER := '9009';
  ELSE
    vBELEGART := '';
    vGEGENKONTONUMMER := '';
```

```
END IF;
    IF (:NEW.GEGENKONTO >= 4000 AND :NEW.
GEGENKONTO < 5000) OR :NEW.GEGENKONTO = 0
THEN
    vSTEUERSCHLUESSEL := '3';
    ELSIF :NEW.GEGENKONTO >= 5000 AND :NEW.
GEGENKONTO < 6000 AND :NEW.GEGENKONTO != 5125
THEN
    vSTEUERSCHLUESSEL := '9';
    ELSIF :NEW.GEGENKONTO = 5125 THEN
    vSTEUERSCHLUESSEL := '20';
    ELSIF :NEW.GEGENKONTO >= 1000 AND :NEW.
GEGENKONTO < 2000 THEN
    vSTEUERSCHLUESSEL := '';
    ELSE
    vSTEUERSCHLUESSEL := '';
    END IF;
    IF :NEW.BETRAGSOLL IS NOT NULL AND :NEW.
BETRAGSOLL != '0' THEN
    vBUCHUNGSBETRAG := :NEW.BETRAGSOLL;
    ELSE
    vBUCHUNGSBETRAG := :NEW.BETRAGHABEN;
    END IF;
    INSERT INTO TBFBDI_SATZ_F_OP(SATZART,INTERN_
VKZ,FIRMENNUMMER,BELEGART,BELEGDATUM,BUCH
UNGSPERIODE,BELEGNUMMER_INTERN,KONTONUMM
ER,GEGENKONTONUMMER,STEUERSCHLUESSEL,STEU
ERSATZ,BUCHUNGSBETRAG,BUCHUNGSTEXT,WAEHRU
NG,FAELLIGKEIT,KURS)
        VALUES('F','0','001',vBELEGART,:NEW.
Rechnungsdatum,'122005',:NEW.Rechnungsnummer,TO_
CHAR(:NEW.KONTONUMMER),vGEGENKO
NTONUMMER,vSTEUERSCHLUESSEL,:NEW.
UstSatz,vBUCHUNGSBETRAG,:NEW.Buchungstext,'EUR',:
NEW.Faelligkeit,:NEW.Kurs);
```

```
    EXCEPTION
      WHEN OTHERS THEN
        NULL;
END TBFBDI_OFFENE_POSTEN_AFT_INS;
/
```

How do I resolve this?

✍ ANSWER

It can only be one of those fields prefixed with a ":". Check their spelling against the table's column names (TBFBDI_OFFENE_POSTEN).

After doing the checking, you need to give the structure of the table 'TBFBDI_OFFENE_POSTEN;
'.

☞ QUESTION **76**

Uploading of data from Oracle database table to an excel file

I am using this oracle version, Oracle Database 10g Enterprise Edition Release 10.1.0.3.0. It is currently connected to the Oracle Database 10g Enterprise Edition Release 10.1.0.3.0 - 64bit Production, with the Partitioning, OLAP and Data Mining options.

I have to upload the data from Oracle database table to an Excel file in a more efficient way, as there might be 500 to 1000 rows in a table which I have to upload into Excel through PL/SQL.

The server is UNIX and client is on windows environment. The problem is to push the data from server to client and show the data in Excel. The whole thing has to be done from Oracle forms-6i.

How do I automate the whole process so that user can do the operation on click of a button?

✍ ANSWER

Just use sqlplus and spool to write out a data file. The sqlplus can run on the client.

Use text_io.put_line command in forms. This will create a comma separated values file which can be used in excel. Simply concatenate the data with commas.

For example: data1ll','lldata2ll',' and so on..

This can be used to create a normal editor file which can be extended in Excel.

☞ QUESTION 77

Dynamic SQL for an IF statement

I'm working on Oracle 7.3

I have a table that contains data that I wish to use to create an IF statement to test against variables in my package.

My table is as follows:

```
create table th_pack_dets_logic
(th_pack_dets_id    number(12,0),
 th_logic_id        number(12,0),
 var_ao             varchar2(3),
 var_statement      varchar2(30),
 var_operator       varchar2(30),
 var_value          varchar2(5),
 var_datatype       varchar2(1),
 userid             varchar2(30),
 timestamp          date)
```

For the purposes of my test I'm using the fields' var_statement and var_value.
These contain the values 'retentioncell' and 5 respectively.

What I want to do is generate the IF statement such as:

If rententioncell = 5 by selecting the information from the table and using that, retentioncell will exist as a variable in my code and will contain a value.

I've been trying to use dynamic SQL to achieve this, but either it cannot be done or I just can't get my head round it.

This is my piece of test code:

declare

```
    cursor c_main is
    select var_statement,
           var_value,
           var_datatype
    from th_pack_dets_logic
    where th_pack_dets_id = 6;

    cur PLS_INTEGER := DBMS_SQL.OPEN_CURSOR;
    fdbk PLS_INTEGER;
    local_var VARCHAR2(200); /* Receives the new value */
    cmdstring varchar2(2000);
    counter number;
    v_test varchar2(50);
    v_test2 number;
    retentioncell number;

begin

counter := 1;
v_test2 := 1;
retentioncell := 1;

    DBMS_SQL.PARSE
    (cur,'DECLARE retentioncell number := :ndec; BEGIN if :
testing = :one then :vstatement := :yfield; end if; END;',2);
    counter := 1;

    for c_rec in c_main
    loop
        dbms_output.put_line(c_rec.var_statement); -- This will
be the text retentioncell
```

```
        DBMS_SQL.BIND_VARIABLE (cur, 'testing', c_rec.var_
statement);
        DBMS_SQL.BIND_VARIABLE (cur, 'one',1);
        exit;
        counter := counter + 1;

    end loop;

    DBMS_SQL.BIND_VARIABLE (cur, 'ndec', retentioncell);
    DBMS_SQL.BIND_VARIABLE (cur, 'vstatement', 'N');
    DBMS_SQL.BIND_VARIABLE (cur, 'yfield', 'Y');

    fdbk := DBMS_SQL.EXECUTE (cur);
        DBMS_SQL.VARIABLE_VALUE (cur, 'vstatement', local_
var);

    dbms_output.put_line(local_var);

    end;
```

If I execute the code as it is ,then I get a numeric or value error which I'm assuming is due to the fact that the if statement is trying to compare the text retentioncell with the value 1 (indeed if I bind 1 to 'testing' then it works fine).

What I wanted to do was dynamically generate an IF statement on the fly by using values from a table. However, as the expression is being treated as a literal rather than the name of a variable I don't believe I can do it. I'll just have to code it longhand.

As for the version of Oracle, I'm just a code monkey working for an employer, so I have no choice on version.

Is there an elternate way of doing this?

✍ **ANSWER**

I believe you are confusing literal values with variable names. You are building an IF statement that attempts to compare a character value to a numeric value which raises an error like so:

```
scott@ORA92> BEGIN
  2   if 'retentioncell' = 1 -- causes error
  3   then null;
  4   end if;
  5  END;
  6  /
BEGIN
*
ERROR at line 1:
ORA-06502: PL/SQL: numeric or value error: character to
number conversion error
ORA-06512: at line 2
```

When you change 1 to 'testing', it eliminates that particular error:

```
scott@ORA92> BEGIN
  2   if 'retentioncell' = 'testing' -- eliminates error
  3   then null;
  4   end if;
  5  END;
  6  /
```

PL/SQL procedure successfully completed.

Although your code may then execute without errors, I doubt

that it is doing what you want it to do. If you could provide a more complete explanation of your overall goal, dynamic SQL may not even be necessary. Also, you definitely need to upgrade. The oldest currently supported version is 9i. Oracle 7 was desupported a long time ago.

You can use your values to build a sql statement string that you store in another variable (v_sql in the example below), then parse and execute that SQL statement string.

```
scott@ORA92> CREATE TABLE th_pack_dets_logic
  2   (th_pack_dets_id     NUMBER(12,0),
  3      th_logic_id          NUMBER(12,0),
  4      var_ao               VARCHAR2(3),
  5      var_statement        VARCHAR2(30),
  6      var_operator         VARCHAR2(30),
  7      var_value            VARCHAR2(5),
  8      var_datatype         VARCHAR2(1),
  9      userid               VARCHAR2(30),
 10      timestamp            DATE)
 11  /
```

Table created.

```
scott@ORA92> INSERT INTO th_pack_dets_logic
  2   (th_pack_dets_id, var_statement, var_value)
  3  VALUES (6, 'retentioncell', 5)
  4  /
```

1 row created.

```
scott@ORA92> SET SERVEROUTPUT ON
scott@ORA92> DECLARE
  2    CURSOR c_main IS
```

```
3   SELECT var_statement,
4          var_value
5   FROM  th_pack_dets_logic
6   WHERE th_pack_dets_id = 6;
7   cur                  PLS_INTEGER := DBMS_
SQL.OPEN_CURSOR;
8   fdbk                 PLS_INTEGER;
9   local_var            VARCHAR2(200);
10  retentioncell        NUMBER := 1;
11  v_sql                VARCHAR2(2000);
12 BEGIN
13  FOR c_rec IN c_main
14  LOOP
15     DBMS_OUTPUT.PUT_LINE ('c_rec.var_statement: '
|| c_rec.var_statement);
16     v_sql := 'DECLARE retentioncell NUMBER := ' ||
retentioncell || ';'
17        || ' BEGIN IF ' || c_rec.var_statement || ' = :one'
18        || ' THEN :vstatement := :yfield; END IF;
19           END;';
20     DBMS_OUTPUT.PUT_LINE ('---------------------------');
21     DBMS_OUTPUT.PUT_LINE ('v_sql: ' || v_sql);
22     DBMS_SQL.PARSE (cur, v_sql, 2);
23     DBMS_SQL.BIND_VARIABLE (cur, 'one', 1);
24     DBMS_SQL.BIND_VARIABLE (cur, 'vstatement', 'N');
25     DBMS_SQL.BIND_VARIABLE (cur, 'yfield', 'Y');
26     fdbk := DBMS_SQL.EXECUTE (cur);
27     DBMS_SQL.VARIABLE_VALUE (cur, 'vstatement',
local_var);
28     DBMS_OUTPUT.PUT_LINE ('---------------------------');
29     DBMS_OUTPUT.PUT_LINE ('local_var: ' || local_
var);
30     DBMS_OUTPUT.PUT_LINE ('---------------------------');
31  END LOOP;
32  DBMS_SQL.CLOSE_CURSOR (cur);
```

33 END;
34 /
c_rec.var_statement: retentioncell

----

v_sql: DECLARE retentioncell NUMBER := 1; BEGIN IF
retentioncell = :one THEN :vstatement := :yfield;
END IF;
        END;

----

local_var: Y

PL/SQL procedure successfully completed.

scott@ORA92>

☞ QUESTION **78**

PARTITION CAN NOT BE SPLIT

I am trying to split my partition as:

ALTER TABLE P_SERVICE
SPLIT PARTITION FB_100000000 AT (100000000) INTO
(PARTITION FB_1204915 tablespace USERS,
PARTITION FB_100000000 tablespace USERS)
UPDATE GLOBAL INDEXES;

100000000 is my high value for FB_100000000. I even tried to give some new high value like 1204925. But I am still getting the error "PARTITION CAN NOT BE SPLIT ALONG THE SPECIFIED HIGH BOUND";

How can I resolve this?

Is my objective possible?

✍ ANSWER

The first version didn't work because you cannot split a partition at its old high value. You need to use a lower value, but not lower than the high value of the next lowest partition.

To quote from an Oracle Error Messages Manual:

"ORA-14080: partition cannot be split along the specified high bound.

Cause: User attempted to split a partition along a bound which either collates higher than that of the partition to be split or lower than that of a partition immediately preceding the one to be split.

Action: Ensure that the bound along which a partition is to be split collates lower than that of the partition to be split and higher that that of a partition immediately preceding the one to be split."

Either you are splitting the wrong partition, or you are splitting it at a value that it does not cover.

```
select PARTITION_NAME, HIGH_VALUE
from user_tab_partitions
where table_name = 'P_SERVICE'
order by partition_position
/
```

To list the partitions and their upper bounds, find the partition immediately above FB_100000000, is its high value >= 1204925"

End of quote.

☞ QUESTION **79**

UTL_FILE handling ISO Latin 1

I need to create a file using UTL_FILE. The file should be created using ISO-8859-1 character set (or ISO Latin 1).

Is there a setting required for this?

How do I create this file?

✍ ANSWER

You should check the character set of your database for a start. Select value from nls_database_parameters where parameter = 'NLS_CHARACTERSET';

The easiest way to test it is to create a test table containing the ISO-1 characters you want, and then dump them to a file using a hex editor, hex or octal dump of the file, to examine the bytes written. Oracle characterset WE8ISO8859P1 is ISO-1. ISO-1 is compatible with Windows CP1252, ISO-15 UTF8 etc.

ISO-1 characters are: http://www.unicode.org/Public/ MAPPINGS/ISO8859/8859-1.TXT

e.g. F7 is DIVISION SIGN, so convert to decimal, then insert using chr() to be safe: insert into mytab values (chr(to_ number('FF', 'XX')), 'DIVISION SIGN');

DECLARE

```
x1 UTL_FILE.FILE_TYPE;
BEGIN
x1 := UTL_FILE.FOPEN('/tmp', 'myoutput', 'W');
for i in (select col1 from mytab order by 1) loop
UTL_FILE.PUTLINE(x1, i.col1||' '||i.descrip);
end loop;
UTL_FILE.FCLOSE(x1);
EXCEPTION
WHEN utl_file.invalid_path THEN
raise_application_error(-20000, 'ERROR: Invalid path for
file.');
END;
/
```

Older versions were limited in what could be written using utl_file. You can write ISO-1 as it is only a single byte characterset.

☞ QUESTION 80

To achieve Parallel Processing using procedure

My requirement is to have an Oracle Procedure. Using the same procedure I need to process around 250k + rows from a table one by one. I am using sun cluster Environment with Oracle RAC

How can I implement this?

✍ ANSWER

If they write in different places, there won't be any real contention here. I would just run them in parallel.

Set job_queue_processes to some number larger then the number of parallel threads you want.

Set job_queue_interval to something reasonable (like 60).

Then simply have a procedure that submits all 5, commits and exits. The 5 procedures will start running within a minute, all at the same time in the background.

If you want to monitor them, use dbms_application_info. set_session_longops so you can see how far they are along.

There is no reason *not to try* in a controlled environment. For example, if you can test it first to make sure there are no conflicts. That of course would be preferable as there may be dependencies you haven't thought about.

☞ QUESTION 81

Capture SQL in trigger

I want to capture the delete statement which is executed over a particular table through the trigger on the table. The problem is my database version is 8.1.6 and the system event ora_sql_txt is not present.

I tried to capture sid through "SELECT sys_context ('USERENV', 'SESSIONID') into nsid from dual;" and join it v$session and v$sql for sql_hash_value-=hash_value or prev_hash_value=hash value, but it does not captures the SQL and I get no_data_found error.
Is there a better way of doing it?

✎ ANSWER

You can't just join v$session, v$sql reliably like normal tables and views because they are constantly changing. Try selecting from each on the views one at a time. Even if you get it to work there in no guarantee that it will be 100% reliable. Check it from dbms_job too. The userenv('sessionid') will not work. Instead, try using sid from v$mystat to get the v$session row.

"select *
  FROM v$session
where sid = (select sid from v$mystat where rownum = 1
)".

☞ **QUESTION 82**

FORALL with EXECUTE IMMEDIATE

I am trying the following:

"FORALL l_loop_cntr IN 1..l_count
EXECUTE IMMEDIATE ' INSERT INTO ' ||c_table || ' VALUES
l_NE_BILL_REPORTS_table (:1) ' USING l_loop_cntr";

My table name is dynamic but it gives an error as follows:

"Compilation errors for PROCEDURE PL_OWNER.TEST_BULK"

Error: PLS-00435: DML statement without BULK In-BIND cannot be used inside FORALL
Line: 27
Text: EXECUTE IMMEDIATE ' INSERT INTO ' ||c_table || '
VALUES l_NE_BILL_REPORTS_table (:1) ' USING l_loop_cntr";

How do I fix this?

✍ **ANSWER**

Try to immediately execute the entire forall block like this:

"SCOTT@ORACLE> drop table myemp;

Table dropped.

SCOTT@ORACLE> create table myemp as select * from emp where 1=2;

Table created.

SCOTT@ORACLE> select * from myemp;

no rows selected

SCOTT@ORACLE> declare
```
  2  p_str long;
  3  d_table varchar2(30) := 'MYEMP';
  4  begin
  5  delete from myemp;
  6  p_str := 'Declare type l_table is table of emp%rowtype;' ;
  7  p_str := p_str||' p_table l_table := l_table();' ;
  8  p_str := p_str||' Begin select * bulk collect into p_table
from emp;';
  9  p_str := p_str||' forall i in 1..p_table.count';
 10  p_str := p_str||' insert into '||d_table||' values p_table(i);
end;';
 11  execute immediate p_str;
 12  end;
 13  /
```

PL/SQL procedure successfully completed.

SCOTT@ORACLE> select empno,ename from myemp;

```
    EMPNO ENAME
--------- ---------
     7369 SMITH
     7499 ALLEN
     7521 WARD
     7566 JONES
```

7654 MARTIN
7698 BLAKE
7782 CLARK
7788 SCOTT
7839 KING
7844 TURNER
7876 ADAMS

EMPNO ENAME

---------- ----------
7900 JAMES
7902 FORD
7934 MILLER

14 rows selected.

SCOTT@ORACLE>".

☞ QUESTION **83**

Oracle date function

I have a question about Oracle date function.

If today is 10-Jan-2006, what function can I use to get the last month end i.e. 31-Dec-2005 and the last quarter end say, 31-Oct-2005?

✍ ANSWER

The answer actually depends on your business logic for last quarter end.

For example:

SQL> ALTER SESSION SET NLS_DATE_FORMAT = 'DD-MON-YYYY'
  2 /

Session altered.

SQL> COLUMN last_month_end FORMAT A14
SQL> COLUMN last_qtr_end FORMAT A12
SQL> SELECT SYSDATE   today
  2 ,   TRUNC(SYSDATE,'MM') - 1   last_month_end
  3 ,   TRUNC(SYSDATE,'Q') - 1   last_qtr_end
  4 FROM   DUAL
  5 /

TODAY   LAST_MONTH_END LAST_QTR_END
--------- -------------- -----------

10-JAN-2006 31-DEC-2005   31-DEC-2005

SQL>

☞ **QUESTION 84**

Bulk select with Dynamic SQL

I was trying to use bulk select with Dynamic SQL. The actual problem is different from the one given below; but it also uses the same logic.

"SQL> CREATE OR REPLACE TYPE TT IS TABLE OF NUMBER;
2 /

Type created.

SQL>
SQL> DECLARE
2 T1 TT ;
3 STR VARCHAR2(200);
4 BEGIN
5 STR := 'SELECT DEPTNO BULK COLLECT INTO :1 FROM
    DEPT' ;
6 EXECUTE IMMEDIATE STR USING T1;
7 END;
8 /
DECLARE
*
ERROR at line 1:
ORA-01745: invalid host/bind variable name
ORA-06512: at line 6"

Why is this error happening?

How do I make this logic work?

🖎 ANSWER

Simply read the documentation and use the right syntax:

SQL> declare
  2   type emp_tab is table of number index by pls_integer;
  3   etab emp_tab;
  4 begin
  5   execute immediate 'select empno from emp where deptno
= :1' bulk collect
  6   into etab using 10;
  7   for i in 1..etab.count loop
  8   dbms_output.put_line(etab(i));
  9   end loop;
 10 end;
 11 /
7782
7839
7934

PL/SQL procedure successfully completed.

☞ QUESTION 85

Inserting and displaying image from database

I have to develop an application of search engine with image.

main_tran Table :

id number pk

log_entery varchar2(4000)

image blob

I want to upload the image with log_entry.

How can I upload image to database?

After uploading into database, how can I display from the database?

I want this kind of o/p:

Id	log_entery	image
1	You r great	img_of_id-1
2	you r too great	img_of_id-2

Where can I find the solution for this?

✎ ANSWER

Use the solution described in Metalink Note #202017.1, or the one below:

Change "num_cgi_vars number;" to "num_cgi_vars number := 0;" in pubowa.sql and reinstall by running owainst.sql.

For anyone not brave enough to change the code, you can run something like this from the session first:

```
DECLARE
    nm      OWA.vc_arr;
    vl      OWA.vc_arr;
BEGIN
    -- initialize cgi environment, then num_cgi_vars will be not
null
    nm (1) := 'REMOTE_ADDR';
    vl (1) := '1.2.3.4';
END;
/
```

☞ QUESTION 86

Error procedure + package variables

I have created 2 packages.

1st:
create or replace package Error_handling as

procedure p_error(error_in in varchar2);

end Error_handling;
/
create or replace package body Error_handling as

stmt number;
proc_name varchar2(50);

ex_null_value exception;
ex_foreign_key exception;
ex_check_con exception;
pragma exception_init(ex_null_value,-1400);
pragma exception_init(ex_foreign_key,-2291);
pragma exception_init(ex_check_con,-2293);

procedure p_error(error_in in varchar2)
is
begin
if (upper(error_in)='TOO_MANY_ROWS') then
raise_application_error('-20001',SQLERRM || '. Error in
Statement: '|| stmt || ' in procedure '|| proc_name || ' !!!');
rollback;
elsif (upper(error_in)='NO_DATA_FOUND') then
raise_application_error(-20002,SQLERRM || '. Error in

statement '|| stmt|| ' in procedure '|| proc_name || ' !!!');
rollback;
elsif (upper(error_in)='DUP_VAL_ON_INDEX') then
raise_application_error(-20003,SQLERRM || '.   Error   in
statement '|| stmt || ' in procedure '|| proc_name || ' !!!');
rollback;
elsif (upper(error_in)='STORAGE_ERROR') then
raise_application_error(-20004,SQLERRM || '.   Error   in
statement '|| stmt || ' in procedure '|| proc_name || ' !!!');
rollback;
elsif (upper(error_in)='VALUE_ERROR') then
raise_application_error(-20005,SQLERRM || '.   Error   in
statement '|| stmt || ' in procedure '|| proc_name || ' !!!');
rollback;
elsif (upper(error_in)='EX_NULL_VALUE') then
raise_application_error(-20006,SQLERRM || '.   Error   in
statement '|| stmt || ' in procedure '|| proc_name || ' !!!');
rollback;
elsif (upper(error_in)='EX_FOREIGN_KEY') then
raise_application_error(-20007,SQLERRM || '.   Error   in
statement '|| stmt || ' in procedure '|| proc_name || ' !!!');
rollback;
elsif (upper(error_in)='EX_CHECK_CON') then
raise_application_error(-20008,SQLERRM || '.   Error   in
statement '|| stmt || ' in procedure '|| proc_name || ' !!!');
rollback;
elsif(upper(error_in)='OTHERS') then
RAISE_APPLICATION_ERROR(-20009,SQLERRM || '. Error
in statement '|| stmt || ' in procedure '|| proc_name || ' !!!');
rollback;
end if;
end p_error;
end Error_handling;
/
After that I created another package with the same package

vars as the error package contains.(stmt,proc_name)

2nd Package: (I will leave the head of the package)

```
create or replace package body test_data as
stmt number;
proc_name varchar2(50);

ex_null_value exception;
ex_foreign_key exception;
ex_check_con exception;
pragma exception_init(ex_null_value,-1400);
pragma exception_init(ex_foreign_key,-2291);
pragma exception_init(ex_check_con,-2293);

procedure test(first in VARCHAR2,second in VARCHAR2)
is
begin
proc_name := 'hello';
stmt := 27;
insert into testtable
(row1,row2)
values
(first,second);
exception
when NO_DATA_FOUND then
error_handling.p_error('NO_DATA_FOUND');
when TOO_MANY_ROWS then
error_handling.p_error('TOO_MANY_ROWS');
when DUP_VAL_ON_INDEX then
error_handling.p_error('DUP_VAL_ON_INDEX');
when STORAGE_ERROR then
error_handling.p_error('STORAGE_ERROR');
when VALUE_ERROR then
error_handling.p_error('VALUE_ERROR');
```

```
when EX_NULL_VALUE then
error_handling.p_error('EX_NULL_VALUE');
when EX_FOREIGN_KEY then
error_handling.p_error('EX_FOREIGN_KEY');
when EX_CHECK_CON then
error_handling.p_error('EX_CHECK_CON');
when OTHERS then
error_handling.p_error('OTHERS');
end test;
end test_data;
/
```

The problem is, if I get an error while executing the test procedure with the insert, the error message from the error procedure seems like this:

"Error in statement in procedure!

The package vars stmt and proc_name have no values. But they should show 27(for stmt) and hello for proc_name"

Is there an example with a setter procedure?

Do I need a better procedure in my exception handling package which gets the variables from the executable package?

Do I need a setter procedure in my executable package, which sets the variable of the error package?

Were can I find an example of setting a variable?

✍ ANSWER

The package-global statement and proc_name in the package error_handling have absolutely no relationship with the two variables in the other package. You should not expect them to interact, simply because their names match. Either provide the stmt and proc_name from test_data as parameters to p_error or create setter-procedures to set the values of the variables in the error_handling package.

I hope this is just an exercise, because the best way to handle this is to drop your error-package and your exception handlers.

For examples of setter procedures search the web. It is a common method. It provides a way to assign values to variables that are hidden to the outside world since they are declared in the package body.

An example is given below:

SQL> create or replace package mypackage
2 is
3   procedure set_myvar
4   (p_myvar in varchar2
5   );
6   procedure mylog
7   ;
8 end mypackage;
9 /

Package created.

SQL> create or replace package body mypackage
2 is

```
3   g_myvar varchar2(100);
4
5   procedure set_myvar
6   ( p_myvar in varchar2
7   ) is
8   begin
9     g_myvar := p_myvar;
10   end set_myvar;
11
12   procedure mylog
13   is
14   begin
15     dbms_output.put_line('Myvar is '||g_myvar);
16   end mylog;
17 end mypackage;
18 /
```

Package body created.

```
SQL>
SQL> exec mypackage.mylog
Myvar is
```

PL/SQL procedure successfully completed.

```
SQL> exec mypackage.set_myvar('great');
```

PL/SQL procedure successfully completed.

```
SQL> exec mypackage.mylog
Myvar is great
```

PL/SQL procedure successfully completed.

You call the setter procedure in your main-package where you now assign values to stmt and proc_name.

☞ QUESTION 87

Occurrence

I have a requirement where in I need to trap duplicate values in the rows, and put the single occurrence by wiping out the dups. My column values are something like this:

'disp latex free free free freetest'
'distilled water water mineral water'
'spread sheet sheet'

I need to have the output like this:

disp latex free freetest
distilled water mineral water
spread sheet

If the occurrence is repeating immediately for the second time, those should be eliminated

Where can I find resources to resolve this?

✍ ANSWER

With the data provided there is only one option:

select 'disp latex free freetest'
from   dual
union all
select 'distilled water mineral water'

```
from   dual
union all
select 'spread sheet'
from   dual
/
```

☞ QUESTION **88**

Trigger code error

I'm trying to put a trigger onto table1 that will eventually cause data to be inserted into table2. My immediate problem is getting the new data to be inserted into variables. Here is an example of what I have:

```
CREATE OR REPLACE TRIGGER tr_table1_insert
AFTER INSERT ON table1
FOR EACH ROW
DECLARE
v_emp1 NUMBER(3);

BEGIN
SELECT :new.emp1 INTO v_emp1;

END;
```

This gives me the following error:
PLS-00103: Encountered the symbol ";" when expecting one of the following:. (, % from

What's wrong with the syntax?

What I'm trying to do is update table1, and then take the difference between the old value and the new value, and insert this difference into table2. The difference between the old salary and new salary does not necessarily need to be inserted into a 2nd table. It could be inserted into another column in the 1st table. Actually, this might be preferable.

For example, let's say we're working with salaries. John Wayne is making $19.00 an hour and gets a raise to $20.00 an hour. I would update the salary column, setting salary = 20.00 where name = 'John Wayne'. Then I want the difference of 20.00 and 19.00, which is 1.00, to be inserted into table2 (say into a salary_increase column where name = 'John Wayne'). I would like to have table2 updated using a trigger on table1 so that it happens as table1 is being updated.

I did a little research, and found that the old.salary and new. salary contain the values that I want, so I tried to simply complete the following expression: v_salary_increase:= new.salary - old.salary; and then insert v_salary_increase into table2. I got a PLS-00201 error saying that 'new.ab' must be declared, so I'm now trying to figure out how to declare it.

✍ ANSWER

Every SELECT statement needs the FROM clause. That is, to correct your trigger, modify the SELECT statement, such as:

SELECT :new.emp1 INTO v_emp1 FROM dual;

Since you didn't provide the complete trigger code, I'd suggest you modify the logic you are trying to implement. Auxiliary variable 'v_emp1' is not necessary. The trigger might look like this, and it will do what you want:

CREATE OR REPLACE TRIGGER tr_tab1_insert
AFTER INSERT ON TAB_1
FOR EACH ROW
BEGIN
    INSERT INTO TAB_2 (col1) VALUES (:NEW.col1);

END;
/Report message to a moderator

This would be just a simple after update trigger. There is no need for any intermediate variables.

```
create or replace trigger table1_trg
after update of salary on table1
for each row
begin
   insert into table2 (name, salary_increase) values (:new.
name, :new.salary - :old.salary);
end;
```

☞ QUESTION **89**

Get the latest records

I am working on a project. The theme is like this: There are messages coming through airlines and stored in the database. There are previous messages also stored. I am just concerned with the new data being inserted. I want to know how to retrieve the latest record through PL/SQL query.

What is the query used in retrieving the latest record from the database?

Currently I am working on a Parser for an Airline. They maintain a database whose columns are 4

Id
Time (that is date format)
message_data (CLOB DATA TYPE)
setterFlag (I guess that's Boolean)

I am writing this Parser in Java. The main problem that is occurring, is whenever any new message is inserted in this table, someone told me that a trigger will invoke. This trigger should get the latest data inserted, and pass this message to the corresponding Parser Program.

It means that whenever a new value is inserted, it should fire a trigger that will pass the most recent message from PL/SQL to Java Program Parser. Then rest of the operation will be done on that particular message.

How do I resolve this issue?

✍ ANSWER

You need a column on which you can sort to be able to return 'the last record'.

This sounds like some sort of message queue, with a (java) listener that should be filled from within a trigger. If you would create a row-trigger (after insert for each row), the pseudo-column: new.id would indicate the primary key of the newly inserted record, whereas: new.message_data would contain the newly inserted clob. This could be sent to the procedure handling the filling of the queue.

So, there is no need for a query.

☞ QUESTION 90

Date problem

I am using one cursor that contains one date column.

Fetch date into one variable on this date, is different with table date.

Why is this so?

✍ ANSWER

This is about a different output format. For example, when retrieving data from the table, you use:

"SELECT TO_CHAR(date_column, 'dd.mm.yyyy') FROM";

Meanwhile, when displaying the cursor variable value, you use something like:

"DBMS_OUTPUT.PUT_LINE(TO_CHAR(cur.date_column, 'mm/dd/yy'))".

If that is the case, simply use identical format in both situations.

☞ QUESTION 91

Returning a Ref Cursor

I tried to fetch the returning cursor but it gave me the following error:

"ORA-06504: PL/SQL: Return types of Result Set variables or query do not match
ORA-06512: at line 9"

How do I fetch the returning cursor into a type?

SQL> create or replace type emp_ty as object(empno number,ename varchar2(20),sal number,deptno number);

SQL> create or replace type emp_nt as table of emp_ty;

SQL> create or replace type dept_ty as object(deptno number,dname varchar(20),emp emp_nt);

SQL> create or replace type dept_nt as table of dept_ty;

```
declare
type empreftyp is ref cursor;
empref1 empreftyp;
v_emp_nt emp_nt := emp_nt();
v_dept_nt dept_nt := dept_nt();
begin
open empref1 for select empno,ename,sal,deptno from emp;
fetch empref1 into v_emp_nt;
close empref1;
end;
```

✍ Answer

There are two things that need to be done. First, your SQL statement needs to use the emp_ty constructor, since you're fetching into a TABLE type, every "row" which is an instance of an OBJECT type (emp_ty). Second, don't forget that you're returning multiple rows here, so you need to BULK COLLECT, i.e.:

```
SQL> declare
 2   type empreftyp is ref cursor;
 3   empref1 empreftyp;
 4   v_emp_nt emp_nt := emp_nt();
 5 begin
 6   open empref1 for select emp_ty(empno,ename,sal,deptno) from emp;
 7   fetch empref1 bulk collect into v_emp_nt;
 8   close empref1;
 9 end;
10 /
```

PL/SQL procedure successfully completed.

☞ QUESTION 92

Use of returned cursor in another PL/SQL proc

I have a procedure like this in package CORP_REPORT:

```
PROCEDURE Confronto
( IN_IDREQUEST IN NUMBER,
CUR_1 IN OUT CORP_REPORT.TCUR_1
)
IS
BEGIN
... do something ...
OPEN CUR_1 FOR
SELECT * from table1, table2, tableEtc..
where <something specific> ;

END;
```

It works perfectly with ORACLE.NET data provider, ADO, Crystal, etc.

In some cases I need to process that data again in PL/SQL, something like this:

```
PROCEDURE NewConfronto
( IN_IDREQUEST IN NUMBER,
CUR_1 IN OUT CORP_REPORT.TCUR_1
)
IS
InternalTCUR CORP_REPORT.TCUR_1;
BEGIN
```

```
EXEC Confronto(IN_IDREQUEST,InternalCUR);

OPEN CUR_1 FOR
SELECT x,y,z
from InternalCUR
where <..other conditions...>;
END;
```

How can this be done?

✍ ANSWER

You can apply the following:

```
PROCEDURE NewConfronto
( IN_IDREQUEST IN NUMBER,
) IS
InternalTCUR CORP_REPORT.TCUR_1;

BEGIN

  Confronto(IN_IDREQUEST,InternalCUR);
  /* internaltcur is now open, since confronto opened it */
  loop
    fetch internaltcur into ....
    exit when internaltcur%notfound;
    <do your stuff>
  end loop;
  close internaltcur;
END;
```

☞ QUESTION 93

Dynamic selection of columns

My table contains 100 columns. I want to enter the number of columns as an input, and that an N number of columns should be displayed from the table. E.g. if I enter 10, first 10 columns values should be printed.

Is this possible using PL/SQL?

If yes, how is it done?

✍ ANSWER

The following is a sample procedure you can copy or duplicate:

```
SQL> CREATE OR REPLACE PROCEDURE get_n_columns
(
 2   p_table_name   IN  VARCHAR2
 3 , p_columns      IN  POSITIVE
 4 , p_rc           OUT SYS_REFCURSOR
 5 )
 6 IS
 7   l_sql    VARCHAR2(32500) := 'SELECT ';
 8 BEGIN
 9   FOR c IN (SELECT  utc.column_name
10          ,      ROW_NUMBER()
11                 OVER (PARTITION BY utc.table_name
```

```
12                    ORDER BY    utc.column_id) r
13          FROM    sys.user_tab_columns    utc
14          WHERE    utc.table_name = p_table_name
15          ORDER BY utc.column_id)
16    LOOP
17       IF (c.r <= p_columns) THEN
18          l_sql := l_sql || c.column_name || ',';
19       ELSE
20          EXIT;
21       END IF;
22    END LOOP;
23    OPEN p_rc FOR RTRIM(l_sql,',') || ' FROM ' || p_table_
name;
24  END get_n_columns;
25  /
```

Procedure created.

SQL> VARIABLE rc REFCURSOR
SQL> EXEC get_n_columns('EMP',4,:rc);

PL/SQL procedure successfully completed.

SQL> PRINT rc

```
    EMPNO ENAME     JOB         MGR
---------- --------- --------- ---------
    7369 SMITH     CLERK      7902
    7499 ALLEN     SALESMAN     7698
```

```
7521 WARD      SALESMAN     7698
7566 JONES     MANAGER      7839
7654 MARTIN    SALESMAN     7698
7698 BLAKE     MANAGER      7839
7782 CLARK     MANAGER      7839
7788 SCOTT     ANALYST      7566
7839 KING      PRESIDENT
7844 TURNER    SALESMAN     7698
7876 ADAMS     CLERK        7788
7900 JAMES     CLERK        7698
7902 FORD      ANALYST      7566
7934 MILLER    CLERK        7782
```

14 rows selected.

SQL> EXEC get_n_columns('DEPT',1,:rc);

PL/SQL procedure successfully completed.

SQL> PRINT rc

```
    DEPTNO
----------
        10
        20
        30
        40
```

SQL>

☞ QUESTION 94

Dynamic insert procedure

I need to insert a record in a table dynamically. A procedure that exists is defined by:

Insert name_table (record rowtype%nametable); that inserts a record without writing to the field of the table.

Is this possible?

How can this be accomplished?

✍ ANSWER

It is possible and here is an example:

SQL> CREATE TABLE t1 (c1 NUMBER, c2 DATE);

Table created.

```
SQL>
SQL> DECLARE
  2   t1_rec t1%ROWTYPE;
  3  BEGIN
  4   t1_rec.c1 := 1;
  5   t1_rec.c2 := SYSDATE;
  6   INSERT INTO t1 VALUES t1_rec;
  7  END;
  8  /
```

PL/SQL procedure successfully completed.

☞ QUESTION **95**

Procedure/Function Execution Time

I wrote a procedure in which multiple DML is performed and it took some time. I want to find the total time the procedure took to execute.

How can I find the total execution time for any procedure or Function?

✎ ANSWER

You can use one of the following approaches:

1. Use dbms_profiler;
2. Enable trace with wait events;
3. If you are executing the procedure from SQL*Plus then before executing it; Set timer on.

Alternatively, you can use DBMS_UTILITY.GET_TIME function in the procedure, before and after the DML operations. The main difference is the execution time.

If you are using SQL*PLUS environment for execution, in addition to "SET TIME ON", give the command: "SET TIMING ON". It will provide you the elapsed time on each execution.

☞ QUESTION 96

Fetch bulk records subjected to very frequent updation

I have a table of 2000 records having around 10 columns. All these records are subjected to very frequent updation say (>=1 second).

I have to fetch all these 2000 records at any instant of time. This happens very frequently.

What kind of approach will be the best solution for this requirement?

✍ ANSWER

Oracle looks after it for you. A SELECT is point-in-time consistent, so you are guaranteed to see a snapshot of the data at the time you started the query.

With 2000 rows you should not have any problem, but with larger volumes you could get a Snapshot Too Old error (search this forum on ORA-1555 if you are interested).

A lakh (also spelled lac or laksha) is a unit in a traditional number system, still widely used in India, Pakistan and Bangladesh, equal to a hundred thousand. A hundred lakhs make a crore.

This system of measurement also introduces separators into numbers in a place that is different from what is common outside India. For example, 3 million (30 lakh) would be written as 30,00,000.

☞ QUESTION 97

Delete Old Records

I want to delete aged (4 months old) records from Materialized view but not from master tables. I have created updateable materialized view in Oracle 9i. I am able to delete aged records from that materialized view, but at next refresh all aged records are again being populated to the Materialized view along with new records.

How do I fix this?

✍ ANSWER

You are doing a COMPLETE or a FAST refresh.

If COMPLETE, then your technique is not going to work. I've never tried this technique, but I thought FAST should work. If it doesn't, try this series of steps:

1. dbms_mview.refresh(user.mv, 'F');
2. Delete rows from MV;
3. ALTER MATERIALIZED VIEW mv CONSIDER FRESH;

☞ QUESTION 98

Oracle + XML

I have a question on Oracle + XML.

I am aware about the procedure using Java but I am not sure about PL/SQL procedures to be followed.

How do I validate XML file against a schema (XSD) using a PL/SQL procedure?

✍ ANSWER

Well, one easy way is to create an XMLTYPE variable which is schema-based (i.e. associated to registered XSD on the database via DBMS_XMLSCHEMA).   If it succeeds it's valid against the XSD.   Or else it'll fail with a *relatively* descriptive error.

Here's an example procedure for doing it (when you've got a CLOB "XML" document):

```
PROCEDURE validate_xml(xml    IN CLOB,
              xsd    IN VARCHAR2 DEFAULT NULL,
              xmlout OUT XMLTYPE)
  AS
  BEGIN
    xmlout := XMLTYPE.CreateXML(xmldata => xml, schema => xsd);

    IF xsd IS NOT NULL
```

```
  THEN
    xmlout.SchemaValidate;
  END IF;
 END validate_xml;
```

As I said, there are many ways to skin this cat like inserting into a table which has a schema-based XMLTYPE column etc.

☞ QUESTION 99

"to_date" behaving differently for 2049 and 2050

I am facing a very peculiar problem in my production as well as testing platforms.

I have a table with the following fields:

Table name: Ams_mt_account
Account_id number(10),
validity_date date,
expiration_date date

How can the behavior of the following 2 queries be explained?

1. select to_date(expiration_date) from ams_mt_account where account_id=7676

This returns 12/4/2049 if the expiration_date is set to 12/4/2049 in the field value for that account.

FYI, to_date is used eventhough the field is date in the table. I cannot change this as of now since it's a production platform and requires some time for change.

2. Select to_date (expiration_date) from ams_mt_account where account_id=7676

This returns 12/4/1950, if the expiration_date is set to 12/4/2050 in the field value for that account.

Is there anything that I can change in the oracle parameters
to get the correct output?

✍ ANSWER

You cannot do a to_date on a field with a datatype date.
Besides that, you should never do a to_date without providing
a format.

It has to do with sliding windows as a result of the Y2K
problem.
Change your nls_date_format from dd-mon-yy (or rr) to dd-
mon-yyyy.
And, yes, do change your code; it contains a bug as it is.

☞ QUESTION **100**

Error while refreshing materialized view through DBMS_MVIEW

I am facing some problem while refreshing the materialized view.

I have one schema FPD_OBJ, on which all the tables are created.

Second schema FPD_SP I have, on which database packages (procedure/functions) are created. On this schema I have created Private synonyms pointing to the tables creates on FPD_OBJ.
GRANTS (SELECT, INSERT, UPDATE & DELETE) have been given to FPD_SP user.

Third schema I have FPD_USER, through which I am executing the stored procedure. EXECUTE privilege has been given to FPD_USER from FPD_SP.

I have a Materialized View (FPD_ACTIVITY_SUMMARY_MV) which is again created on FPD_OBJ schema. Now one of my stored procedures (in FPD_SP) executes DBMS_MVIEW.REFRESH ('FPD_ACTIVITY_SUMMARY_MV','C'); to refresh the materialized view, after some data processing. This stored procedure is being executed from FPD_USER schema. The other entire procedure works fine except for this one, and it gives error â œORA-01031: insufficient privileges. I have given all the privileges (SELECT, INSERT, DELETE, UPDATE) on this Materialized View to FPD_SP schema, but still it gives me an error. If I comment this code then the stored procedure works fine.

Is there any other privilege that has to be given to FPD_ USER or FPD_SP, so as the REFRESH happens through the procedure?

Is there any other way to REFRESH the view through procedure keeping it in FPD_OBJ schema?

✍ ANSWER

A complete refresh will issue a TRUNCATE table statement, which is not covered by SELECT, INSERT, UPDATE, DELETE.

The manual says:

"To truncate a table or cluster, the table or cluster must be in your schema or you must have DROP ANY TABLE system privilege".

Either grant DROP ANY TABLE priv to FPD_SP, or move the proc and the table to the same schema (which is what you have done).

INDEX

Attention SAP Experts

Have you ever considered writing a book in your area of SAP?
Equity Press is the leading provider of knowledge products
in SAP applications consulting, development, and support.
If you have a manuscript or an idea of a manuscript, we'd
love to help you get it published!

Please send your manuscript or manuscript ideas to
jim@sapcookbook.com – we'll help you turn your dream
into a reality.

Or mail your inquiries to:

Equity Press Manuscripts
BOX 706
Riverside, California
92502

Tel (951)788-0810
Fax (951)788-0812

50% Off your next
SAPCOOKBOOK order

If you plan of placing an order for 10 or more books from www.sapcookbook.com you qualify for volume discounts. Please send an email to books@sapcookbook.com or phone 951-788-0810 to place your order.

You can also fax your orders to 951-788-0812 .

Interview books are great for cross-training

In the new global economy, the more you know the better. The sharpest consultants are doing everything they can to pick up more than one functional area of SAP. Each of the following Certification Review / Interview Question books provides an excellent starting point for your module learning and investigation. These books get you started like no other book can – by providing you the information that you really need to know, and fast.

SAPCOOKBOOK Interview Questions, Answers, and Explanations

ABAP	-	SAP ABAP Certification Review: SAP ABAP Interview Questions, Answers, and Explanations
SD	-	SAP SD Interview Questions, Answers, and Explanations
Security	-	SAP Security: SAP Security Essentials
HR	-	mySAP HR Interview Questions, Answers, and Explanations: SAP HR Certification Review
BW	-	SAP BW Ultimate Interview Questions, Answers, and Explanations: SAW BW Certification Review
	-	SAP SRM Interview Questions Answers and Explanations
Basis	-	SAP Basis Certification Questions: Basis Interview Questions, Answers, and Explanations
MM	-	SAP MM Certification and Interview Questions: SAP MM Interview Questions, Answers, and Explanations

SAP BW Ultimate Interview Questions, Answers, and Explanations

Key Topics Include:

- The most important BW settings to know
- BW tables and transaction code quick references
- Certification Examination Questions
- Extraction, Modeling and Configuration
- Transformations and Administration
- Performance Tuning, Tips & Tricks, and FAQ
- Everything a BW resource needs to know before an interview

mySAP HR Interview Questions, Answers, and Explanations

Key topics include:

- The most important HR settings to know
- mySAP HR Administration tables and transaction code quick references
- SAP HR Certification Examination Questions
- Org plan, Compensation, Year End, Wages, and Taxes
- User Management, Transport System, Patches, and Upgrades
- Benefits, Holidays, Payroll, and Infotypes
- Everything an HR resource needs to know before an interview

SAP SRM Interview Questions, Answers, and Explanations

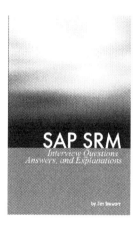

Key Topics Include:

- The most important SRM Configuration to know
- Common EBP Implementation Scenarios
- Purchasing Document Approval Processes
- Supplier Self Registration and Self Service (SUS)
- Live Auctions and Bidding Engine, RFX Processes (LAC)
- Details for Business Intelligence and Spend Analysis
- EBP Technical and Troubleshooting Information

SAP MM Interview Questions, Answers, and Explanations

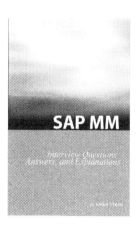

- The most important MM Configuration to know
- Common MM Implementation Scenarios
- MM Certification Exam Questions
- Consumption Based Planning
- Warehouse Management
- Material Master Creation and Planning
- Purchasing Document Inforecords

SAP SD Interview Questions, Answers, and Explanations

- The most important SD settings to know
- SAP SD administration tables and transaction code quick references
- SAP SD Certification Examination Questions
- Sales Organization and Document Flow Introduction
- Partner Procedures, Backorder Processing, Sales BOM
- Backorder Processing, Third Party Ordering, Rebates and Refunds
- Everything an SD resource needs to know before an interview

SAP Basis Interview Questions, Answers, and Explanations

- The most important Basis settings to know
- Basis Administration tables and transaction code quick references
- Certification Examination Questions
- Oracle database, UNIX, and MS Windows Technical Information
- User Management, Transport System, Patches, and Upgrades
- Backup and Restore, Archiving, Disaster Recover, and Security
- Everything a Basis resource needs to know before an interview

SAP Security Essentials

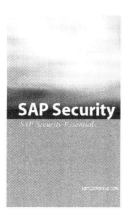

- Finding Audit Critical Combinations
- Authentication, Transaction Logging, and Passwords
- Roles, Profiles, and User Management
- ITAR, DCAA, DCMA, and Audit Requirements
- The most important security settings to know
- Security Tuning, Tips & Tricks, and FAQ
- Transaction code list and table name references

SAP Workflow Interview Questions, Answers, and Explanations

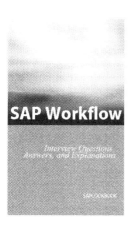

- Database Updates and Changing the Standard
- List Processing, Internal Tables, and ALV Grid Control
- Dialog Programming, ABAP Objects
- Data Transfer, Basis Administration
- ABAP Development reference updated for 2006!
- Everything an ABAP resource needs to know before an interview

www.ingramcontent.com/pod-product-compliance
Lightning Source LLC
Chambersburg PA
CBHW051227050326
40689CB00007B/834